THE IRISH POLITICAL ELITE

Studies in Irish Political Culture 4

THE IRISH POLITICAL ELITE

A. S. COHAN

GILL AND MACMILLAN

First published in 1972
Gill and Macmillan Limited
2 Belvedere Place
Dublin 1

and in London through association with the
Macmillan
Group of Publishing Companies

7171 0538 5

Cover designed by Graham Shepherd

Printing history:
10 9 8 7 6 5 4 3 2 1

Printed and bound in the Republic of Ireland by
Cahill & Co. Limited Dublin 8

For Bessie and Dottie

Acknowledgements

I am most grateful for the help and co-operation that was extended to me when I was resident in Ireland in 1968-69. Both Brian Farrell and Tom Garvin have been excessively generous to me in terms of time and patience. Additionally, our mutual friendships have grown since that time, and they have been a source of great support to me. With regard to this work, Mary Dowey, Ireland's finest example of Women's Liberation in action, has invariably been correct in her suggestions and criticisms.

At the University of Lancaster, Professor P. A. Reynolds of the Department of Politics has been most encouraging to me at all times. In addition, Professor P. Nailor has, on occasion, read bits and pieces and offered valuable suggestions.

While grateful to these people for all that they have offered to me, I alone must take responsibility for the findings and conclusions in this work.

Contents

1

Introduction: The Passing of the Revolutionary Elite

The beauty of the Irish countryside and the much heralded charm of the people are aspects of life that clearly set Ireland apart from other states. But other factors may be isolated which underline Ireland's similarity to other societies. To the political scientist the political system bears a striking resemblance to other political systems both in structure and process. In fact, the study of the Irish political system and political culture becomes significant only when placed in relation to systems such as that of the United Kingdom—the model from which the Irish system is derived—and several of the smaller European democracies such as Denmark, Norway and Switzerland. With the political patterns that are observed in many of the Irish-dominated big city machines, there are aspects of Irish politics that resemble even the United States.

Further, Ireland was among the first of the post-revolutionary societies to emerge in the twentieth century as well as the first state to mount an ultimately successful guerrilla war against a colonial power. Thus, it is a country with similarities to the developing revolutionary systems of Africa, Asia and Latin America.

Ireland has effectively been an independent state for over fifty years. From both social and political standpoints, patterns have occurred that could develop in the more recently independent states of Asia and Africa when as many years have elapsed since independence. While they may seem to have very little in common, it is only in the Soviet Union and Ireland that enough time has elapsed to witness the clear transition from revolutionary to post-revolutionary, and effectively non-revolutionary society. This study will focus on one aspect of that transition in Ireland. It examines the

1

changes that have occurred in the composition of the political elite since independence from Great Britain was achieved.

The members of the revolutionary elite in Ireland shared one characteristic. Each seemed to have had a deep devotion to the concept of a politically and culturally independent state. Many of the revolutionary fighters were introduced to the military aspects of the coming battle with the English through classes in Irish culture and language conducted mainly by the Gaelic League. The result appears to have been a deeply held sense of national identity that took precedence over more pragmatic considerations such as close economic ties with the British.

Despite the continued tension that has resulted from the still very real problem of partition and the continued civil disorder in the North, a great deal has altered in the Republic. The contemporary political elite is characterised by its pragmatic outlook, especially in economic matters. Ireland is closely tied to its traditional enemy, the United Kingdom, in its political and economic life and is looking to its coming European Economic Community membership which two of the three major parties support.

This study is concerned with those factors which might explain this changed orientation on the part of the political elite. Specifically it asks whether any real differences—other than that of revolutionary participation—are to be found between the revolutionary and post-revolutionary elite that might explain this shift from cultural nationalism to overriding pragmatism, especially in economic matters.

In this work, then, we are examining two elite generations. Here we have special reference to (a) a group that participated in the revolution and (b) one which did not take part in that event. The concept of the elite generation is not related to the passage of a set number of years. Instead, it refers to elites during 'varying phases of social adjustment'.[1] Hence, a group that participated in the revolution is considered the revolutionary elite. All others, whether young people or adults during that era, will be considered post-revolutionary.

One of the critical underlying assumptions of the field of comparative politics is that among the various political systems similar patterns are likely to occur. Although they will reflect certain factors which are unique to the particular system—certain cultural aspects and historical patterns will occur in one system and not in another—these patterns can nevertheless be expected to occur within each system. Political scientists such as David Easton, Gabriel Almond, Herbert Spiro and Karl Deutsch have each developed models of the political system which, they have suggested, may be applied to virtually any situation in which the process of authoritative decision-making is occurring. This could refer to interactions in the small group, the village, the trade union, the city or the state. While there are differences among the various models, each is based on a common acceptance of the ability to compare.

This assumption of comparability is not above criticism. The models of the political system that have been developed so far may indeed allow for comparability at a rather high level of generality, so high indeed that the models tend to have reduced usefulness. The social scientist must be wary or he may fail to identify factors which are peculiar to a particular system that may well be rooted deep in the past and which, in fact, hold sway over events that are occurring in present times. The models provide only a framework for analysis. A clear example of this emerges when examining the problems and the civil disorder in Northern Ireland. An understanding of current difficulties would be incomprehensible without some appreciation of the separate lines of development that have taken place between the Catholic and Protestant groups. The dependence upon class explanation is insufficient. In the North, at least two political cultures may be located. On one side, history and tradition have made the Republic the object of loyalty of the large Catholic minority of the population. As MacDonagh has stated, religion and nationality become intertwined in nineteenth-century Ireland.[2] On the other side the United Kingdom is viewed as the object of loyalty by those

3

descendants of the settlers who came from England and Scotland. Other points of view may also be located. The critical consideration is that the models do not give us the clues that may be needed to examine such differences. Rather, the researcher must supply the essential details.

With these reservations, the concept of comparability is accepted in this work. The desire to compare presents us with considerably more interesting reasons for examining the political elite of Ireland. If one accepts the status of a science of politics, then by studying facets of political life in several systems, propositions and hypotheses may be derived that can be tested when examining other systems. With some regularity and direction in findings one may then make predictions about what might be expected to occur in other systems which are demonstrating similar patterns of development. Here, Ireland is a most interesting system. As stated, it was one of the first of the post-revolutionary societies. Thus, by investigating what has occurred in Ireland we may see how other countries may be expected to evolve.

The Passing of the Revolutionary Elite

Herbert Spiro, in an article which attempted to develop a model of the political system, suggested the following hypothesis for dealing with the transition from the revolutionary to post-revolutionary period in any given society. He stated :

Members of any non-stagnant political system change their estimates of the most important problems it faces. If they start, for example, by considering solution of the problem of independence from outside rule most important, as colonial independence movements have, the initial style of the system may be more or less violently ideological. Once independence is achieved, leaders identified with solution of the problem of colonialism will be regarded as most authoritative in all phases of the political process. If the independence movement develops successfully into a new political system, its style will add elements of

4

pragmatism and legalism, as concern shifts to flexibility and stability, the original problem having been solved efficiently and effectively, i.e., in an acceptable fashion.[3]

For Spiro, the attainment of legitimacy is a particular type of problem. Once legitimacy is attained by the new regime, different goals are set. Such was the case with Ireland. Once the revolutionary generation passed from the political scene during the politically confusing decade between 1949 and 1959, a more pragmatic group emerged. A revolutionary generation is bound by the vision that it has of what the revolution ought to attain. The sacrifices it made are expected to provide the fertiliser for the new unfettered society. A group that is not brought up during the revolutionary era is likely to be concerned with the mundane patterns with which revolutionary leaders do not seem to have concerned themselves, either in Ireland or in other societies.

A number of theories to explain the change from revolutionary to post-revolutionary society have been elaborated. One political scientist, John Kautsky, has written about the shift that occurs from revolutionary to post-revolutionary or managerial elites in modernising societies.[4] By this he means that in the aftermath of a revolution the group that finally takes power is frequently incapable of coming to grips with the kind of problems that are likely to arise during that period.

In a remarkably clear and concise study of the Chinese cultural revolution,[5] R. J. Lifton has focused on Mao's fears that after his own death the revolution will die as well. For Mao, it has been vital to turn the post-revolutionary era into 'a state of politicised straight-and-narrow moral earnestness pursued with unrelenting passion'.[6] This strong commitment is difficult to develop among those who had no part in the great struggle. The cultural revolution in China may be seen as that ultimate effort to restore the sanctity of the revolutionary goals. Chinese contempt for the post-revolutionary return to normality in the Soviet Union demonstrates what the Chinese leadership has wished to avoid for itself. The Soviets are referred to in a derogatory manner as revisionists.

5

One notices a comparable revisionism in Ireland. In interviews with numbers of the elite who had participated in the revolutionary era, the end of partition and the revival of the Irish language were still perceived as the major problems with which Ireland ought to be concerned. The loss of a 'national culture' was thought to be highly undesirable. Among the post-revolutionary elites, economic matters—the ending of emigration, association with the European Economic Community, greater industrial development—were considered most important.

From this very brief description it can be seen that the cultural nationalists who founded such movements as the Gaelic League and Sinn Féin have given way to the pragmatic young men of the Lemass and Lynch regimes. How complete this shift has been may be seen in the relative strength of the Fianna Fáil hardliners with regard to the Northern question and the moderates such as Lynch and Hillery. The anti-Free State party of the Civil War and after has, in a sense, recognised the existence of the North *de facto* as a separate entity and, while supporting reunification, is realistic about its possibilities. The younger men know about the revolutionary era through family experiences, not through actual participation. The resulting outlooks between revolutionaries and post-revolutionaries are bound to differ.

In order to examine more precisely why this particular shift has taken place, this work concentrates on the social backgrounds of the members of the political elite because generally 'the study of the social background of decision-makers almost always proceeds on the often unstated assumption that the key to behaviour lies in the group's socio-economic background'.[7] Actually, very little in the field of political studies has attempted to link social background characteristics with attitudes. Further, 'attitudinal studies frequently assume that what the respondent says holds considerable relevance to his future behaviour, though very little work has actually been done on relationships between saying and doing'.[8]

Attitude should not be taken to mean the same thing as

behaviour. How a person acts may or may not reflect how he actually feels about a given issue. This work is concerned with social background and behaviour because it holds that through this type of study the reasons for the change in behaviour of the members of the elite will become obvious. If the backgrounds of the revolutionary group are very different from those of the post-revolutionary group then the variation may explain the alternative modes of behaviour. If differences are to be found in social class background and educational experience, then these might help to explain the goals pursued by the two groups. If, however, no differences exist other than the experience or lack of experience of the revolution then it might be concluded that the revolutionary experience and what moved people to participate in the revolution has led to one set of goals, i.e., cultural nationalism, while non-participation has led to a more pragmatic outlook.

The study of backgrounds has further significance. Even if it is unable to explain attitudes or behaviour, it nevertheless indicates what a particular society values in its leaders. This is especially valuable when studying changes that have occurred over a long period of time. By studying the social background of two different elite generations we may understand changes in the value system as well as changes in the goals of the political leaders. Such is clearly the case in Ireland and this will be demonstrated in later chapters.

In order to set the subject matter in perspective, the first part of this work is devoted to a brief analysis of the changes between revolutionary and post-revolutionary elites. The next chapter examines the usefulness of studies of the political elite as well as some relevant aspects of theories as to who its members are. This will preface an identification of the members of the Irish political elite and the reasons why this particular identification has been used. Suggestions will also be made concerning how the elite group may be expected to change.

The composition of this group will be explored with regard to social background, education, occupation and socialisation—the way in which one is brought into the political

7

culture. Attention will be directed to the differences that have emerged between the revolutionaries and post-revolutionaries with special attention directed to different recruitment patterns. By recruitment patterns we mean the ways in which individuals become members of the political elite.

From this, certain conclusions will be drawn that may be applicable to other societies. Where relevant, references will be made to other societies in which certain political patterns bear similarity to those in Ireland. Finally, we will focus on the political direction in which the elite seems to be heading, given the continued pressure of events in the North.

NOTES

[1] Harold Lasswell, Daniel Lerner, C. Eaton Rothwell, *The Comparative Study of Elites,* Stanford 1952, 9.

[2] Oliver MacDonagh, *Ireland,* Eaglewood Cliffs, N.J. 1968, 11.

[3] Herbert Spiro, 'Comparative Politics: A Comprehensive Approach', *American Political Science Review,* LVI (September 1962), 577.

[4] John Kautsky, 'Revolutionary and Managerial Elites in Modernising Regimes', *Comparative Politics,* I, No. 4 (July 1969), 441-467.

[5] See Robert J. Lifton, *Revolutionary Immortality: Mao-Tse-Tung and the Chinese Cultural Revolution,* Pelican Books 1970.

[6] *Ibid.,* 136.

[7] Carl Beck and James Malloy, 'Political Elites: A Mode of Analysis'. Paper presented to the Sixth World Congress, *International Political Science Association,* Geneva 1964, 6.

[8] Donald Searing, 'The Comparative Study of Elite Socialisation', *Comparative Political Studies,* I (January 1969), 494.

2

The Identification of the Political Elite

Within the field of comparative politics the study of political elites is not new. The problems of leadership fascinated even the earliest political philosophers. Aristotle, for example, dealt with the question of leadership by suggesting three qualifications for the individuals who filled the highest offices in the state. He maintained that they ought to be loyal to the existing constitution, a requirement which demonstrates great understanding of the danger of a revolution or a conspiratorial coup. He believed that these men needed to have strong administrative capacity and, finally, that they should demonstrate virtue and a sense of justice. He recognised that concepts of virtue and justice might well differ according to the differences in the values of the various systems, but within the context of those systems, virtue and justice must be displayed.

What is remarkable about the Aristotelian formulation is that the problem that he raised—the need to understand how a community's values define the direction a leadership group may take—is still central to the study of politics and is still an area of analysis that is most difficult to handle.

Aristotle and the vast majority of those who followed him posed two questions. First, they asked: who should rule? They were concerned with the kinds of qualities individuals who were to be entrusted with the lives of the citizens of the state ought to have. Then they asked: how should they rule? What methods should they use which would best meet proper standards of justice? For nearly three thousand years these questions predominated. But in the field of politics during the period of the late nineteenth and early twentieth centuries, a new group of political thinkers appeared. With the works of sociologists such as Marx, Mosca, Pareto, and Michels, the questions posed were altered substantially.

The new sociologists abandoned the ' should ' and asked instead 'who does rule?' and 'how do leaders rule?' But underlying both approaches was a most salient point. In every society someone or some group or some combination of groups rules. The particular form that the leadership group takes may vary, but that someone rules is usually taken for granted. Marx, for example, related leadership to property ownership. The leadership formations came from the propertied class. Mosca wrote the following passage which is perhaps the most frequently cited in the description of leadership. He said:

> In all societies—from societies that are very meagrely developed and have barely attained the dawnings of civilisation, down to the most advanced and powerful societies—two classes of people appear—a class that rules and a class that is ruled. The first class, always the less numerous, performs all political functions, monopolises power and enjoys the advantages that power brings, whereas the second, the more numerous class, is directed and controlled by the first, in a manner that is now more or less legal, now more or less arbitrary and violent, and supplies the first, in appearance at least, with material means of subsistence and with instrumentalities that are essential to the vitality of the political organism.[1]

The view that Mosca held may be a bit simplistic. The rather rigid division that he established may not hold up under close scrutiny. But the question, 'Does anybody rule?' is not asked at all. There exists an assumption that in any society, at a given moment in time, somebody or some group rules. Society without rulers seems unreasonable to all but a few hardy anarchists.

But the answer to the question, 'Does anybody rule?' does not tell us who does rule. Regardless of the particular constitutional form that the state may have, those who are legally supposed to rule are not always those who actually

10

make the decisions that are vital for a society. Nowhere in the American constitutional formula are listed the industrialists and military men who do exercise considerable influence over policy. In fact, no study of the American policy process would be complete without an understanding of the role that these people with only limited or no official governmental capacity play. Similarly the governmental framework prescribed in the Irish constitution ignores not only the role of major interest groups but also the political parties.

In recent years the study of bureaucracies has commanded considerably more attention because it is here that the real policy constraints may frequently be found. One cannot study the French political system, for example, without having some understanding of that system's bureaucracy. It may have been the relative independence of the bureaucracy which provided stability in the period of chronic governmental uncertainty and change, at least until 1958.

In many of the developing countries it is through the military offices that power is exercised. Ireland is one of the few new states to have escaped this trend. Further, in a number of new African states the leaders of particular tribal groups are considerably more important and influential within the tribes than are many of the 'national' leaders. In Yugoslavia local leaders may have greater support than the national leader. Countries such as Ceylon, Israel, Spain, Ireland and Italy contain leadership situations in which researchers could examine the influence of the religious community and discover whether people of high religious station do act as decision-makers.

The question that remains concerns who does actually rule. While the primary concern of this work is the influence of certain events on behaviour patterns—or social goals—of the political leaders, identification of the elite is a significant problem. In fact, it has been one of the thorniest problems to face researchers in this field.

Lasswell and Kaplan's definition of the elite as 'those with the most power in a group'[2] is relatively straightforward. It

11

assumes that in any polity there will be leaders and followers. Those that lead—and they represent a rather small proportion of the population—are those with the most power. But the simplicity of this definition is deceptive. Indeed, how is one able to locate those with power in a group? How is a term such as power defined? Does power refer to the ability to coerce or persuade? By what criteria does one measure the amount of power a person has? These questions are raised to demonstrate how difficult it is to identify the elite according to the power leaders are said to have.

The problem of the identification of leaders is best typified by two works in the field. In the first, *Community Power Structure*,[3] Floyd Hunter, who examined a southern city in the United States, posed the question, who has power? By interviewing a number of people he constructed a list of those in the community who—ostensibly—were the most powerful. His elite tended to be economic, political and social leaders. Having power in one area was related to having power in another. Hunter saw the structure of society as a pyramid with the leadership forming the top part.

Robert Dahl, on the other hand, in *Who Governs?*[4] has argued that power does not reside in individuals. Instead, different groups were able to exert influence at different times depending on the particular issue. Groups that might be affected by a decision reached on a particular issue will act to sway that decision in one direction or another. If the group has no interest in the issue it will not act. Thus Dahl sees power as the result of interactions between or among individuals or groups. To look for a permanent elite group which has interest in every issue is, according to Dahl, a futile exercise.

The type of elite group or groups that may be found in a particular community ought to be considered an empirical question. Leadership formations are likely to be more structured in some communities than in others. Assuming that is the case, how is it possible to identify the issues that may arise or the groups in the particular community that have the authority to reach decisions?

12

In a most creative article Peter Bachrach and Morton Baratz[5] have argued that the authors of the various works which deal with the identification of leadership have made the mistake of beginning their studies by examining 'the issues rather than the values and biases that are built into the political system and that, for the student of power, give real meaning to the issues which do enter the political arena.'[6] Before examining the types of issues that may arise and the groups involved in the decisions that resolve them, we must understand the constitutional, legal and other restraints which circumscribe the process of decision-making and, even more important, the issues that are unlikely to arise because of the values (social as well as legal) of the system.

All the works cited contain vital points that enable us to delimit our areas. Hunter is undoubtedly correct when he implies that if various roles in a society—such as Taoiseach—have high status then the populace will expect those who fill such roles to make the authoritative decisions for the society. Because such decisions emanate from high office, they are likely to be obeyed. Dahl also makes a major point when he argues that no single leader or group is likely to be concerned with the entire range of issues that might arise in the community. Potentially, the number of issues that might arise is infinite, even in a relatively small society such as Ireland. Bachrach and Baratz make a significant contribution when they maintain that before one can speak about issues and leaders one needs to know the particular values of the community. In order to examine the contribution each author has made, the role that the Catholic Church plays in Ireland will be studied.

For many years now the dissemination of birth control information and the sale of birth control devices have been prohibited by law. This is not to suggest that such information and devices are absolutely unavailable in Ireland, for if a woman knows the right doctor, the pill is available. Furthermore, the border between the North and the Republic is easily crossed, even in these tense days, and in the North family planning advice is readily available. This, of course, benefits the more comfortably-off section of the population.

As greater knowledge about birth control or family planning has become widespread a greater demand for more information and devices has developed. The question of birth control is an issue within the Church, and much of this uncertainty is reflected in the society. While this more widely felt demand for access to information about birth control devices is growing, there is no such development of a demand for legal abortion. It would seem that this would come under the heading of what Bachrach and Baratz have called the non-issue, i.e. a non-debatable value in the society.

The Church need not enter into the question of legalised abortion. As the chief educator of society, the Church has participated in the creation of values that are widely held. These values limit the possibility of issues arising when Church doctrine is relatively clear in the matter and when nothing conflicts with it. The Church need not intrude in the political sector because the politicians who are legally responsible for deciding such issues happen to hold the same values and are not likely, therefore, to push for a change in the law with regard to abortion.

Additionally, the Church, as Dahl would say, is unlikely to hold an interest in all issues that arise in Irish society. Any number of problems will arise—such as fishing rights once Ireland is associated with the European Economic Community, regional development in the West, expansion of the port of Dublin—that do not directly or indirectly involve the Church.

But in those areas in which the Church might hold an interest, some change may be expected to occur. It is increasingly obvious that it is far too simple a conclusion to hold that if the Church has generally opposed the introduction of birth control devices and information concerning contraception, such changes cannot take place. A more widely travelled part of the population, greater availability of information in books and magazines from outside the Republic, possibly a less religious younger segment of the population, and continued economic pressures, have all combined to enable groups to place certain demands upon the government. Such demands call for the alteration of the law which prohibits the sale of devices and the distribution of birth control information in the Republic. The overwhelming majority of the population may still oppose such a change, but a growing segment of the population has made demands for alteration of the existing laws. This can be seen in defiant trips to the North by women's groups to purchase contraceptives and import them illegally. It can also be seen in the outcry over the ban on birth control advice when a new gynaecological hospital opened in Dublin. Furthermore, Family Planning Clinics operate advisory services, apparently without interference.

Still to be taken into account is another consideration that will, in time, become even more significant. There has been a growing pressure for liberalisation of controls in certain areas—such as family planning and divorce laws—because of the situation in the North. A committee composed of members of the Dáil of all parties suggested changes in sections of the Constitution (written in 1937) as far back as 1966. These changes, not in the least radical, are only now being considered seriously. If the government holds to a rigid, strongly doctrinaire position with regard to the birth control information issue, then the attacks that are made upon the government of the Republic (and the Republic itself) by the militant Northern Protestant groups might be justified. Of course, here the government must tread softly because a change in the Constitution—which would be necessary to alter the ban on divorce—would require a popular vote, and the government must make certain that it could achieve the necessary majority.

In any event, we see here a problem that involves a clash of values. On the one hand, to date Catholic doctrine is reasonably clear with regard to birth control—although not universally supported within the Church. On the other hand, the desire for a 'reintegration of the national territories' is very much a credo of the Republic. So strong has this desire been that in 1937, when the Constitution was written, the goal was institutionalised in that document itself. When such values are in conflict, as they very clearly are in this situation, some alteration must be expected. This will be considered in the conclusion.

Here Hunter's findings have special significance. At some point, it would seem, only the highest authority—a permanent decision-making group that by virtue of its status is called upon to make final choices on major issues—can settle the dispute that is to be found between these two social values. Those who contribute that authority and are able to make that final determination will constitute our political elite group.

Once the prevailing values of the community are broadly identified, it is then possible to identify those 'with the most power in the group'. Where we utilise such a general definition of the elite, a definition that may be applicable to any society, without actually specifying who has the most power—we are setting a conceptual definition. When we try to locate who actually has such power and suggest that persons A, B, and C are powerful, then we are utilising what is called the operational definition. It is relatively easy to say that the elite are those with the most power in the group. It is not quite so simple to specify who actually has the power. No operational definition will be completely satisfactory as any two researchers will have a tendency to look at a particular community in a somewhat different manner. This demonstrates how imprecise our science of Politics still is.

Before we can examine the reasons for different goals between the revolutionary and post-revolutionary political elite groups, we must first specify what we mean by the political elite in Ireland. A general level of agreement could be reached by first specifying the government. Lasswell, Lerner and Rothwell have suggested :

The search for political elite may well begin with what is conventionally known as the government. *Conventionally speaking,* government is the institution which is so named by the community in question. Functionally, however, only the institution which makes the severely sanctioned choices

16

can qualify. Since the decision-makers are not necessarily known at the beginning of research the investigators can select government in the conventional sense as a convenient starting point.[7]

The government in Ireland has probably played a more vital role than, we shall say, the government in the United Kingdom, because it is related to a more homogeneous society, a smaller society, and, above all, a post-revolutionary modernising society. The role that the government was forced to play was magnified many times by the problems of the Civil War, the Anglo-Irish trade war of the 1930s, the strains resulting from the I.R.A. and the Blueshirts, the effects of the emergency period of neutrality in World War II, the lack of industrial growth and low investments in the early days of the state, and the period of economic difficulty following World War II in the late 1940s and the early 1950s. Only a reasonably powerful government could hope to deal with these types of problems.

This is not to suggest that the others are without influence. We have already noted the significance of the Church in Irish life. In an agricultural country such as Ireland, farming organisations must be considered somewhat influential. When issues arise which involve the farm community, the organisations that represent the farmer are likely to play an active part in the final determination of policy. Surely this is a major consideration in the negotiations with the European Economic Community. Discussions are likely to involve the Minister for Agriculture, the department, the secretary of the department and, very frequently, interested T.D.s. Further, it is unlikely that the government—except in times of emergency such as characterised the first forty years of independence—will altogether ignore the wishes of organisations which represent many people on whom the government relies heavily for its electoral support.

Those individuals who lead the state-sponsored bodies must be included in a very broad study for they direct significant areas of Irish life. How much influence has Bord Fáilte, the tourist board, for example, when a major area of potential resort land is earmarked for industrial development? Can an organisation which is responsible through its promotions for bringing so much foreign capital to Ireland each year be ignored? Aer Lingus must also have great influence in those areas in which it is interested. Occasionally Bord Fáilte and Aer Lingus conflict as in the case of United States airlines being permitted to fly into Dublin. Here it is the government which becomes the arbiter. How influential was the Electricity Supply Board when its members decided to build an office block in central Dublin, a decision which doomed another street of Georgian houses? Surely those who lead such organisations must be considered among the most influential in the state within the particular area in which they have a stake.

But we are not looking at those who might have a say in particular issue areas. Instead, the individuals who have access to decisions on a continued basis in broader areas of the political life in the Republic form our political elite group. In the Irish context, the government is particularly appropriate as a starting point. Far more than in the larger and more complex British system, the government in Ireland has been forced, through the nature of the social system itself and certain events, to play the dominant role in political life in Ireland.

A concise statement of the significance of the Irish government—the Cabinet—is provided by Chubb. In dealing with that body he points to the multiple roles of cabinet members or party leaders, government ministers, and department heads:

It is this combination of positions of leadership in the majority party or parties as a whole, in the dominant party group, and in the administration which goes far to explain the pre-eminent position of the Cabinet in the process of government. To quote Bagehot . . . the Cabinet is a 'link which fastens, a buckle which joins' . . . [in Ireland] it is more, for its members do not only in their persons join

18

but co-ordinate party, parliament, and administration by their leader's role in each of these important institutions of government. Moreover, they do not share this leadership. There are few, if any, party leaders outside parliament; there are none in the parliamentary party, for we do not have a strong parliamentary committee system with powerful committee chairmen or rapporteurs as in the United States or some European countries : there are none in the departments for members of the government are themselves the department heads.[8]

Accepting this analysis, it was determined that the following should be included in the group that we refer to as the political elite in Ireland.

1. All individuals who have served as government ministers between 1919 and 1969. The group between 1919 and 1922 refers to those individuals who were leaders of the republican government.
2. All individuals who served as parliamentary secretaries in the governments since 1922.
3. All individuals who have served in the Labour-Fine Gael 'shadow groups' since 1965. This group was added in order to have a wider view of contemporary individuals who are potentially members of the political elite.
4. All individuals who have served as Attorney-General since the foundation of the state in 1922.
5. All persons who have served as Speaker of the Dáil or Senate. While of little significance today, these offices had some impact in the formative years of the state.
6. Within this elected group a final figure is added, the President of the Republic. This adds only Douglas Hyde to the list since the other Presidents had both been government ministers.

The total number of elected members of the elite is 130. Most of the analysis, however, concentrates upon the first three categories. The latter three are not continually involved in the decision process. Thus the effective number will be 109.

This group, however, is not really complete. From the statement by Professor Chubb, one might be left with the impression that the higher civil servant is not particularly influential in the making of policy. In a number of interviews with civil servants and ministers the suggestion was made that the importance of a secretary (the permanent head of the department) is inversely related to the importance or strength of the ministers in charge of that department. Through interviews with others and personal observation this has been found to be inaccurate, or at least an over-simplification with too many exceptions for comfort. Frequently, an active minister has a very influential secretary heading his department. Consider the case of Industry and Commerce when Seán Lemass was minister and John Leydon was secretary.

In a highly legalistic definition the roles of civil servants are described:

> The normal roles of the civil servants in relation to their ministers are (a) to advise them in regard to policy and the manner in which the minister's statutory functions are to be exercised and (b) to implement the policy as laid down by statute and by ministerial directions. The advisory function is ordinarily exercised by senior civil servants, who are therefore in a position to exercise some influence on policy decisions made by ministers or the government; the civil servant's functions are, nevertheless, advisory, and the power of decisions remains a ministerial one.[9]

Only one secretary has ever been removed from office for overstepping the perceived boundaries of the office. In general, the rules of professionalism and neutrality are scrupulously observed. It was found that interviews with departmental secretaries which strayed from the work of that particular department were likely to be ended quickly. Realistically, however, it is the secretary who presents the minister with the various alternative policies, and it is a frequent practice of the secretaries to consider the political implications of a programme as well as the social and economic implications.

In one interview, a high-ranking civil servant remarked that he felt that perhaps the most important problem to be faced by Irish political leaders is the need to decide who should make the decisions. Should decisions be made by the civil servants or by the parliamentary representatives of the people? Obviously, the role played by the parliamentary representatives—we are speaking here of the non-minister—is minimal when compared to the influence of the high-ranking civil servant. Thus this work includes information concerning the socio-economic background of all secretaries of departments since 1923; some of it is derived from interviews with these men. This adds 64 to the elite group and raises the total number of members of the political elite to 194.

In Ireland the political elite has a considerable sway over policy. But the reasons for this strong hold ought to be understood in terms of the country itself and its history.

Ireland is not a large country either in area or in population. In terms of population it is not half as large as London. The Republic contains approximately three million people, nearly a million of whom reside in the Dublin area. The road trip from Dublin to any part of Ireland takes no more than five hours.

As far as the governmental structure of Ireland is concerned local government is weak, and the central government is strong. Decisions that are reached in Dublin can affect the people in Kerry rather more quickly than if Ireland were a large state. It would be correct to assume that the significance of the national administration has increased the authority of the ministers. But more than size and structure explains the pre-eminence of the national government. Surely one could reasonably expect that the various groups have some impact on the government.

In numerous interviews members of the political elite and other political commentators were asked to describe the role that the interest and pressure groups played in the state. All who answered this question argued that these groups had not had the impact upon the national political system that similar groups did in other systems such as Great Britain or the United States. Two explanations were generally offered for the minimal role played by these groups.

In the first instance, the Civil War brought about a distinct political cleavage in the society. It was so clearly defined that it has tended to override other possible lines of cleavage such as that which might exist between the farm and city dweller or high and low income people. One member of the elite remarked that his reason for belonging to a particular party was because his father had done so as a result of Civil War considerations, not as a result of other policy or ideological considerations. He believed that his son would probably have more freedom than he did in party selection but not necessarily a totally free choice.

A second reason revolves about the kinds of problems that Ireland faced through most of the first fifty years of her existence as an independent state. The world depression did not spare Ireland. This was followed by the Anglo-Irish trade war which began after de Valera assumed power in 1932. Simultaneously with the Anglo-Irish trade war was the dual challenge to the authority of the state by both the Blueshirts and the I.R.A. This type of stress may be understood by considering how far the present Government may allow the I.R.A. free action in the Republic before it decides that the I.R.A. is undermining state authority.

Close upon the settlement of the trade war and the destruction of the Blueshirts and quashing of the I.R.A. came the period of neutrality in World War II. This period, as well as what preceded it, led to a high degree of population mobilisation which had the effect of strengthening an already strong Cabinet. Thus, Ireland has been a country in which the politicians have governed, and in which interest groups have not been as active as they might have been had the events described not occurred.

This may be the in the process of changing. New groups are growing and old groups are gaining strength as the Civil War enmities lessen with the passage of time. Party loyalty is coming to be based on factors other than the side taken during the 1922-23 Troubles. The Taoiseach, Mr Lynch, does not have the political party background that Messrs Blaney and Boland have, yet it is Lynch who leads the Republican party. In the not-too-distant future the analysis of the role of interest groups will undoubtedly be a fruitful topic for research. At present there are numerous indications that the various groups will no longer be content to play the largely quiescent role that they have played in the past.

But it will be several more years before the lines of development become clear. Already the business community is emerging as one area of potential pressure. Foreign investors will have a profound influence on policy. Farming groups, as always, are bringing demands to bear on the government. However, at the current time, the student of Irish politics who appreciates how far-reaching the government's strength actually is has a fair understanding of who makes the critical decisions in the country. For now, it is the government that has such authority and uses it in both day-to-day life and in the various crises that arise.

NOTES

[1]Gastano Mosca, *The Ruling Class,* ed. and revised by Arthur Livingstone, trans. by Hannah D. Kahn, New York: McGraw-Hill Book Company 1959, 50.

[2]Harold Lasswell and Abraham Kaplan, *Power and Society,* New Haven 1950, 201.

[3]Floyd Hunter, *Community Power Structure,* Chapel Hill 1953.

[4]Robert Dahl, *Who Governs?* New Haven 1961.

[5]Peter Bachrach and Morton Baratz, 'The Two Faces of Power', *American Political Science Review,* LVI (December 1962), 947-952.

[6]*Ibid.,* 950.

[7]Harold Lasswell, Daniel Lerner, C. Eaton Rothwell, *The Comparative Study of Elites,* Stanford 1952, 8.

[8]Basil Chubb, *The Government: An Introduction to the Cabinet System in Ireland,* 2nd ed. Dublin 1968, 9.

[9]Ian Finlay, *The Civil Service,* Dublin 1966, 21.

C

3

The Social Composition of the Irish Political Elite

The social composition of the political elite indicates what the general populace values in its leaders. In a country such as the Soviet Union it is not surprising that the leaders claim working class rather than another type of background. In Ireland, sports heroes tend to do relatively well in politics as a result of the esteem in which people hold their sports figures. And so it is with any political community. The person whose background is contrary to the system values is not likely to be the person who will emerge as one of the leaders. A first step, then, in an understanding of the Irish political elite involves the general description of what this group comprises.

In this chapter, all 194 cases will be studied; however, they will be broken down into three groups. The first group comprises the 109 who fit into the elected elite category. The remaining groups are (1) the Speakers of the Dáil and Senate and the individuals who have served as Attorney-General who do not necessarily serve as members of the Dáil—bringing their number up to 130 (these individuals also fall into the elected elite category), and (2) the civil servants who add another 64 for a total of 194 cases. Table 1 contains a breakdown of the attributes of the members of the political elite that are discussed in this chapter. The table is divided into 130 cases (elected) and 64 cases (civil servants).

Social Background and Demographic Characteristics

A first series of questions about the background of the political elite deals with the place of birth of individual members. This information is significant for several reasons.

24

TABLE 1

The Irish Political Elite: Socio-Demographic Characteristics of Elected Members and Civil Servants

Variable	(N=130) Elected	(N=64) Civil Servants
Demographic:		
Subject born in Ireland	123 (95%) 1 missing	54 (98%) 9 missing
Subject born in Republic	116 (90%) 1 missing	48 (87%) 9 missing
Subject born in town with 1,500 or over	70 (57%) 7 missing	42 (82%) 13 missing
Subject born in Dublin	27 (22%) 5 missing	13 (25%) 11 missing
Education:		
Primary education or no formal education	33 (27%) 7 missing	6 (10%) 7 missing
Secondary education	20 (16%) 7 missing	16 (28%) 7 missing
Primary degree or higher	58 (47%) 7 missing	15 (26%) 7 missing

The total for primary, secondary, and university education does not total 100% because excluded were those who attended technical or teachers' training schools

Socialisation: (Revolutionary) Revolutionary Participant	57 (45%) 2 missing	12 (20%) 4 missing
Civil War Participant	45 (35%) 2 missing	6 (10%) 6 missing
Arrested (by Irish and/or English)	18 (38%) 2 missing	6 (10%) 6 missing
Volunteers	50 (39%) 1 missing	5 (9%) 6 missing
Sinn Féin	57 (45%) 1 missing	8 (14%) 6 missing

TABLE 1 (continued)
The Irish Political Elite: Socio-Demographic Characteristics of Elected Members and Civil Servants

Variable	(N=130) Elected	(N=64) Civil Servants
Socialisation:		
G.A.A. Member	38 (32%) 12 missing	4 (8%) 16 missing
Gaelic League	49 (42%) 12 missing	10 (22%) 18 missing
Relations in Dáil and/or Senate	36 (28%) 3 missing	3 (5%) 1 missing
Relations in the Elite	16 (13%) 3 missing	3 (5%) 1 missing

Given the fact of heavy emigration, such information reveals whether individuals return to their ancestral or parental home. Additionally, it determines the location of birth within Ireland. The Republic maintains that the northern six counties are part of the whole but artificially divided. If that is the case, then a number of the members of the political elite should be from the North. A third question deals with whether the membership of the elite reflects the urban-rural distribution of the entire population of Ireland.

Six (6 per cent) of the 109 elected individuals were born outside Ireland (this refers to all 32 counties). The inclusion of the other 83 cases added only one more to the list of those born elsewhere. In all, there were 10 missing cases; thus, out of 184 cases, 7 (4 per cent) were born some place other than Ireland. This number is very small, but among those individuals who were not born in Ireland were Eamon de Valera (U.S.A.) and Gerald Boland (England), an active revolutionary, the son of a revolutionary who helped found the G.A.A. and the father of Kevin Boland, a minister who served in the Lemass and Lynch regimes. The younger Boland resigned both his Cabinet office and his Dáil seat in opposition to the government policy toward the North. The significance of birth outside of Ireland as a factor in the marginality of the members of the revolutionary elite will be discussed later.

The smallness of the number of individuals born outside of Ireland indicates that those who leave tend to do so permanently, and those who become a part of the political elite have been socialised within the Irish system. Both de Valera and Gerald Boland were brought to Ireland in very early childhood and were educated in the Church-State school system of Ireland. They were also active participants in a number of nationalist organisations and have never thought of themselves as anything other than Irish.

Considering the Republic, 12 of the elected 109 members of the political elite were not born in the 26 counties. Eliminating the 6 that were born outside of Ireland, 6 (6 per cent) were born in the North. Of 184 cases (10 missing cases) with the inclusion of civil servants and Speakers and Attorney-Generals, a total of 20 were born outside of the Republic with 13 coming from the North. This accounts for some 7 per cent of the total elected and appointed elite. Seven of the civil servants including T. K. Whitaker were from the North. While this figure is slightly higher than the elected elite only, the difference is not significant.

These figures indicate that in spite of the constitutional and nationalist claims to the oneness of Ireland, there is a separation between North and South that is not only political. Although the North contains approximately 35 per cent of the total Irish population, in the political elite of the Republic, it has produced merely 7 per cent. Generally, those individuals who came from the North were in the original revolutionary movement and became involved in political events prior to the advent of partition. Among the individuals were Ernest Blythe and Seán MacEntee. Thus, the political elite is one which is Irish born, and, more specifically, born in the 26 counties. Now that a border exists between North and South, the political elite is totally southern in its composition. No member of the post-revolutionary elected elite has come from the North.

A more even division is to be found between those of urban and rural birth. The Irish census takes the figure 1,500 as the dividing line between an aggregate town and aggregate rural area. Freeman has suggested that many of what the Irish consider urban places would be considered villages in England.[1] Nevertheless, given the Irish context which is traditionally rural, the Irish census configuration seems reasonable and is the standard employed in this work.

Of the 109 elected members of the elite, 60 (58 per cent, 5 missing cases) were born in urban areas. Utilising 194 cases with some 20 missing cases, 112 of the remaining 174 (64 per cent) were born in urban areas. The civil servants are considerably more urban in background. Taking into account 13 missing cases, 42 (82 per cent) were born in urban areas. The political elite is generally more urban in its make-up than the general populace. In 1926, the first year in which the Free State census was taken, only 32 per cent of the entire population was urban, while in 1966 this figure had increased to 49 per cent. Although the percentage of the general population which is urban is not as high as the comparable group within the elite, there has been a steady increase over the years. This over-representation of the urban areas is not unique to Ireland and indicates the possibility of a greater political awareness on the part of those raised in urban areas, as well as a better understanding of political events as a result of clearer communication channels.

Where the members of the political elite come from in Ireland is an interesting question if differences in attitude reflect differences in the birthplace of the individual. In this section we examine the Dublin figures as an example of the representativeness of the political elite. Among the 130 elected members, 27 (22 per cent, 5 missing cases) were from the Dublin area. Thirteen (25 per cent, 11 missing cases) of the civil servants were from Dublin. This approximates to the actual percentage of the national population in the Dublin area. In 1926 the Dublin population was 17 per cent of the total. In 1946 it was 22 per cent, and in 1966 it represented 28 per cent. The population of Dublin has increased over the period that the population of the country generally has been decreasing.

The figures indicated also that the political elite is generally

28

representative of the county distribution of population. Only one county, Offaly, has produced no members of either the elected or the appointed elite. Another county, Leix (Laoghis), has produced a higher number of the political elite than other counties of comparable size, including the O'Higgins family. This may be a more competitive county than others politically, and its larger number of members in the political elite is elected rather than appointed (5 of 6). Additionally, in many of the elections since 1922, Leix and Offaly have been tied together in one constituency, and those who have come from Leix have apparently had greater success in elections than those in Offaly.

Religion

The religious make-up of the political elite is similar to the general population which is nearly 96 per cent Catholic. Within the elected elite the figure is 96 per cent while among the civil servants the figure is 97 per cent (2 non-Catholics, with 4 missing cases). With the overwhelming preponderance of Catholics religion does not appear to be a major issue. Few Protestants seek public office, but if a larger number were to participate, there could conceivably be some resentment. In 1969, however, a Protestant, Erskine Childers, became the Tánaiste (Deputy Prime Minister) in the new Lynch regime, and since the founding of the Free State, Protestants have served in the different governments with little, if any, notice taken. Considered alone, this may have no specific importance, but when compared to the situation in Northern Ireland where, although comprising some 35 per cent of the population, Catholics have been systematically excluded from the governments, Protestant participation in the Republic is remarkable.

A rather interesting feature of the Irish political elite is how few members belong to any religious organisation. An assumption was made that the degree of religiosity of individuals in the elite could be measured by determining how many belonged to organisations such as St Vincent de Paul

29

Society, Knights of Columbanus, Legion of Mary and the Ancient Order of Hibernians. However, the membership in these organisations was very slight indeed. If it is assumed that affiliation with these organisations is a mark of religiosity, then the members of the Irish political elite are not particularly religious. An alternative suggestion simply states that these organisations do not draw men with particularly deep religious conviction; rather, these organisations are alternative outlets to fairly ambitious individuals who may not have had success in political areas. Further, members of the political elite do not perceive them to be necessary for political advancement.

Locality

For those who served in the Dáil, the question was asked whether the individual served in the district in which he was born and/or raised. This was done as a measure of localism. Eighty-two (75 per cent) of the 109 elected members of the political elite served in their home districts. When the number was increased to 130 cases, it was found that 78 per cent served the home district. These findings indicate the strong degree of localism in the Republic. Compared to Britain, the Irish figure is considerably higher. This localism, as shall be seen, is more characteristic of the post-revolutionary members of the elite.

Age

With regard to the age when entering public life, the civil servants were not included as most entered at age nineteen upon completion of secondary school. Only the 109 elected members of the elite were considered. Information was available for 43 of the revolutionary participants and 59 of the post-revolutionary figures. There is no real difference between the two groups with regard to the age upon entering the Oireachtas. The largest number entered between ages 30 and 39 in both; however, it must be remembered that the revolution preceded the establishment of the Dáil by several years, and those who entered the Dáil when it was founded had been active revolutionaries, i.e. nationally known figures such as ministers would be, rather than local politicians.

A survey of the age of entry to the elite is also somewhat confusing. Among the revolutionary group, the typical entrant to the elite was in the age range 40 to 54, while among the post-revolutionary group the usual age of entry was between 35 and 49. To conclude, however, that age of entry into the elite is lower in the post-revolutionary group is not valid. In 1922, with the split in Sinn Féin, the republican group was excluded from the government. This delayed by 10 years the entry into the political elite of the de Valera-led Fianna Fáil group. Fianna Fáil then served virtually unchanged from 1932 to 1959. After Mr Lemass became Taoiseach, a new Fianna Fáil group came into the elite, and their ages were generally between 30 and 44. It is significant that Fianna Fáil did not produce a middle group. The revolutionary participants served for such a long period (27 years) that young, ambitious politicians in the middle period (1940-59) had no access to office and faded from the scene leaving room for the still younger politicians who were available when the revolutionary group finally passed from the scene.

Thus, in spite of the similarity, one may conclude that taking into account the ten year delay of Fianna Fáil's entry into the early elite, the revolutionary elite did have a tendency to enter the national political elite at a younger age. Here, as with the age of entry into the Oireachtas, the revolutionary figures had been prominent nationally for a number of years prior to their entry into the political elite. This, however, is not true of the contemporary group. Although the 1969 Fianna Fáil administration was comprised of young men, this was made possible by the extraordinarily long service of the revolutionary participants which eliminated access to office for individuals who may have comprised a middle group.

Education

A study of educational achievement among members of the political elite reveals in part the value that the system places

31

on education as well as the status of the type of education received. Further, high educational achievement and the type of education received indicates whether attendance at a particular school is helpful in the attainment of elite status as well as the social class of the individual. In Ireland the latter is especially clear because education above primary level was not free, and students from the lower income families are not in a financial position to attend the upper level schools. Whether the schools charge fees may also be immaterial since the member of the lower class family may be expected to contribute to the home. Hence, children of the lower classes leave school after completing the required primary grades and either learn a trade or, in some cases, emigrate.

Forty-eight (44 per cent) of the 109 elected members of the elite attended university. While there are six missing cases among the 109, it is assumed that they did not attend university since the lack of such information would certainly be indicative of non-attendance. Of the 48 that attended a university, 4 did not complete their degrees. Instead they became lawyers and took courses at university level in concert with their legal work. A university degree is not required to become a lawyer.

Forty per cent of the individuals in the elected elite received at least the B.A. In addition, 4 are in the category of having attained the LL.B. or the Higher Diploma in Education, an advanced qualification which permits the individual to teach in a secondary school—the National, or primary, school teacher is not required to hold a university degree. There are 3 M.A.s among the elected elite and one Ph.D., James Marcus O'Sullivan, who served in the Cosgrave administration. University education in Ireland is achieved by some 4 per cent of the general population.[2]

When including the civil servants, Attorney-Generals, and the Speakers of the two houses of the Oireachtas, a total of 73 (40 per cent) of the elite (180 cases, 14 missing cases) completed university degrees. While those who have served as Attorney-General generally displayed a high level of educational achievement, civil servants did not. Only 15 (26 per

32

cent, 7 missing cases) of the civil servants attained the B.A. Where civil servants added to the level of educational achievement is in the category of completion of secondary school. Twenty (16 per cent, 7 missing cases) of the 130 elected members of the elite completed as much as secondary school. Among civil servants this number was 16 (28 per cent, 7 missing cases).

While university attendance denotes higher social class, which university an individual attended also provides insights into his background. Trinity College, Dublin, has traditionally been associated with the Protestant ascendancy. The National University of Ireland, while non-sectarian, has been associated with the Catholics and, more specifically, University College, Galway, has been associated with Fianna Fáil, and University College, Dublin, with Fine Gael. Of the 44 university graduates in the elected group (109), 26 (59 per cent) attended University College, Dublin. When the number is increased to 130, 60 graduated from a university. Of this group, 34 (57 per cent) attended University College, Dublin. The number of members of the political elite who attended Trinity College, Dublin, is very small. Of the 44 elected members of the elite who graduated from a university, 6 (14 per cent) attended Trinity. When using 130 cases, the total is lowered to 10 per cent since none of the added group attended Trinity. Only 2 civil servants were Trinity students (one of whom, Thekla Beere, was a woman and a Protestant). This latter appointment was described as satisfying two demands with one person.

In examining the educational background of members of the political elite, some attention was directed to the question of which primary and secondary schools were attended. Interest was focused on the Christian Brothers schools and Clongowes Wood College.

Within the political elite, a substantially higher percentage of civil servants went to Christian Brothers schools than did members of the elected group. During the course of the research it had been remarked several times that the Christian Brothers schools were training grounds for future civil

33

servants. Background characteristics certainly tend to support this assertion.

A further assertion that was heard fairly frequently stated that when the de Valera regime came into power in 1932 following the Cosgrave (Cumann na nGaedheal) administration it was 'only a change from government by Clongowes men to government by Christian Brothers men'.[3] This, of course, was a suggestion that a middle and upper-middle class group was being replaced by a lower class group. With regard to the elected members of the political elite, the evidence is not terribly strong. While it is true that in the Cosgrave administration, James Burke, Patrick McGilligan, J. Marcus O'Sullivan, James Fitzgerald-Kenney and Kevin O'Higgins attended Clongowes, a rather higher representation than in the Fianna Fáil government that followed, six members of the Cosgrave administration attended Christian Brothers schools —including Cosgrave. Additionally, of those who attended Clongowes, only Kevin O'Higgins may be said to have been a leading figure in that first government. Although Patrick McGilligan may also be considered a prominent figure, he did not have the status that O'Higgins did.

Occupations

Dealing with occupations of the members of the political elite, the civil servants were not included. While some of the civil servants were trained for occupations other than the one they eventually pursued, once they entered the civil service it became their permanent career. Practised occupation other than political career is what is considered. There are, however, several instances in which the individual member of the political elite has claimed politics as the only profession. In those cases, that was considered the occupation pursued. (See Table 2.)

Taking into account missing cases 13 (12 per cent) of the elected 109 members of the elite were actually farmers. When Speakers of the Dáil and Senate and Attorney-Generals were added, the total number was brought up to 16 (13 per cent). In 1960 that part of the population engaged in farming comprised 31 per cent of the population. This figure marks a decrease in the percentage of the population engaged in agriculture. But as an occupational group farmers have always been under-represented in the Irish political elite. The Irish case, however, is not untypical of other systems. The agricultural career is not as significant as are others in this predominantly agricultural country, at least insofar as the members of the political elite are concerned.

Most highly valued are professional occupations which are divided into two categories. The first category includes non-university teachers, engineers, chemists, auctioneers and accountants. In the second and higher category are the university personnel. Also included in the second category are the medical doctors, those in legal professions (both barristers and solicitors), and economists. In the 1966 census, of those gainfully employed the professional and technical groups comprised nearly 8 per cent of the total work force. Of this group, 19,852, or 22 per cent of the professional and technical work force, were engaged in religious vocations. Thus, at least one in five professional people in the general population is a priest or nun.

TABLE 2

The Irish Political Elite: Occupation of Elected Members

Occupations	N = 130
1. Agricultural	16 (13%)
2. Artisan	3 (2%)
3. Skilled and Unskilled Labourer/and Union Official	8 (6%)
4. Business and General Merchant	13 (11%)
5. Journalistic—Artistic	7 (6%)
6. Civil Service	5 (4%)
7. Managerial	6 (5%)
8. Professional	66 (53%)
	124 (100%)
	6 missing cases

35

The number of members of the political elite involved in professional work is considerably greater than that part of the general population. Of the 109 elected members, 46 per cent are, or have been, engaged in professional occupations. When the number is increased to 130, the number of professionally employed is greater still, comprising 53 per cent of the total. This is explained by the inclusion of individuals who have served as Attorney-General, all of whom were in legal professions.

The higher percentage of professional people in the political elite is not exceptional in Ireland. Other studies have shown the same tendency in different systems. What is remarkable in Ireland is that in this post-revolutionary society there is virtually a total lack of military men in the political elite. With only two exceptions, Generals Richard Mulcahy and Seán MacEoin, no members of the political elite were career officers in the armed forces. Even referring to Mulcahy and MacEoin as career officers is questionable as Mulcahy left the service in 1924 and MacEoin, who ran for President against de Valera in 1959, considered himself a blacksmith, the trade he had learnt, not an army man. Since the army crisis in 1924 the army in Ireland has been very small, and, with few exceptions (in the 1930s), insignificant in Irish political affairs. The only real prominence that the Irish army has managed to achieve has been its role in United Nations peace-keeping operations. But this, too, has involved only a small number of individuals and has no particular relevance to Irish domestic political affairs.

Another interesting feature of the Irish political elite is the lack of businessmen in the group. This is surprising because of the inclusion in the merchant category of publicans. This may be explained by a real problem encountered in the analysis of occupations in Ireland. A number of individuals who practise one occupation may be engaged in another as well, especially as a merchant (either grocer or publican). In any event, it could be reasonably expected that more businessmen will find their way into government, especially in Fine Gael or Fianna Fáil.

Generally, however, the significant feature of the Irish political elite, insofar as its make-up is concerned, is its under-representation of the agricultural sector and very high percentage of professional people as opposed to their rather low percentage within the general population of those gainfully employed.

Socialisation

Attempting to isolate those experiences in the individual's life which may be crucial to an understanding of his socialisation is an important part of this work. Few members of the political elite, for example, belonged to the organisations which may have been indicative of religious conviction. But religion plays a major role, perhaps the major role, in the socialisation process as evidenced by the significance of the religious values in limiting issues and in their incorporation into legal framework in the state, the 1937 Constitution.

Other factors—events, organisations, and family ties—may also be considered as important in the socialisation process. Given the more than fifty-year period that has elapsed since 1919, the members of the political elite have gone through substantially different 'initiations' into political life. Sixty-nine of the 188 cases for whom there was information were participants in the revolutionary period while others lived through the period but did not participate or were not born until after that event and the Civil War were over.

The most tumultuous period in modern Irish history occurred between 1916 and 1923 when the revolutionary activity reached its peak. Upon the settlement of the revolution a civil war broke out. Of the 109 elected members of the political elite, 49 participated in the revolution. Assuming that the two missing cases did not participate, 45 per cent of the political elite thus had revolutionary experience. The assumption concerning the two missing cases is based upon the conclusion that since the revolutionary experience has been related to success in office-seeking, such information would not be withheld from a biography. With 130 cases, 45 per cent still participated. When civil servants are included, those participating drop dramatically to 36 per cent. Many of the civil servants in the early period did not take part in the political events at all in spite of the difficulties. Only 12 (19 per cent) of the 64 highest civil servants ever had revolutionary experience. The tradition of non-involvement in politics of civil servants would explain the small number who participated.

The Easter Rising of 1916 initiated the revolutionary era, and participation in that event, which resulted in the martyrdom of all of the commandants with the exception of de Valera (he was still an American citizen at the time, and the British chose not to execute him), was considered a special badge of honour. Twenty (18 per cent) of the 109 elected members of the political elite participated in the Easter Rising. With the inclusion of all other members of the elite, only 24 (12 per cent) took part in that event. Among the participants in the Easter Rising were Eamon de Valera, Seán Lemass (as a very young runner), Seán T. O'Kelly, Seán MacEntee and James Ryan—basically the large percentage of members of the 1932 Fianna Fáil government. In the previous government W. T. Cosgrave, Desmond Fitzgerald, Richard Mulcahy, Ernest Blythe, Joseph McGrath and Michael Hayes had taken part in the Rising.

One individual interviewed suggested that every man in Dublin then living now claims to have been at the G.P.O. Another person who has now some rather harrowing experences to tell about the ordeal may not have been there at all. When a later member of the elite went to this individual's house to tell him of the Rising the latter was not inclined to join in the fighting. So certain was he, in fact, of the futility of the Rising that he lent his gun to the person who tells the story. Time, it would seem, had added considerably to the glamour of the event. Only 3 civil servants participated. One of these men, Seán Nunan, later accompanied de Valera to the United States. The Rising was localised in Dublin, and many of those living outside of the capital attempted to reach the scene but were cut off by the action of British troops in surrounding the city.

The Civil War, a completely Irish affair, involved 41 (38

38

per cent) of the 109 elected members of the elite. When all 194 cases are considered, the number of participants increases to 51 but the percentage drops to 26. Only 6 of the 64 civil servants took part in it, once again because of the tradition of non-involvement. The number of participants among the elite may be inflated with the inclusion of a number of Free State government members in the category of participant. Several members of the political elite were too young to participate in the early stages of the War of Independence but were old enough to become active in the Civil War.

A total of 54 were arrested sometime during the revolutionary and Civil War period when all members of the political elite are considered. Forty-eight (38 per cent) of the 130 elected members of the elite were imprisoned. Prison experiences varied considerably, and several were arrested a number of times both by the British and the Irish, and a large number were deported to Great Britain for a period. The great majority of the early Fianna Fáil leaders experienced arrest by both of these parties. Only 6 civil servants were arrested, but this follows from the small number of civil servants who participated in the revolution and Civil War.

The revolutionary front organisation was Sinn Féin, a relatively small organisation until the British incorrectly referred to the 1916 Rising as the Sinn Féin rebellion. In their biographical sketches, 50 (46 per cent) of the 109 members claimed membership in the organisation. With 130 cases 57 (45 per cent) belonged to Sinn Féin. Only 8 (14 per cent) civil servants were members.

A slightly smaller number of the political elite were Volunteers. Forty-three (39 per cent) of the 109 elected members belonged to that organisation. When the remainder was added to include Speakers, Attorney-Generals, and civil servants, a total of 55 (29 per cent) belonged to the Volunteers. The Irish Revolutionary Brotherhood (I.R.B.), that organisation which infiltrated the Volunteers and took credit for the Easter Rising, claimed only 18 (17 per cent) of the elected 109, and with the addition of the remainder of the political elite, taking into account 10 missing cases, there were only 23 (13 per cent)

39

members of the I.R.B. Only 4 civil servants ever belonged to the I.R.B. Among these was P. S. O'Hegarty, a noted historian. The Catholic Church disapproved of the Fenian movement and the 1867 Rising, and the I.R.B. as well. This disapproval may have been at least partially responsible for the small membership. Once again, the small civil service membership is tied to the lack of a civil service role in the revolutionary effort.

The break with the past after the revolution was almost totally complete since the membership in the old Irish parliamentary party did not enter into the post-revolutionary elite. Of the 109 elected members of the political elite, only one—James Dillon—claimed membership in the parliamentary party (he never served in the British Parliament), and he was a very young man at the time, about eighteen years old. Membership in the Republican Dáil, the body that was founded in 1919 as the new Irish government, was held by 23 (21 per cent) of the members of the 109 elected members of the elite. When increased to 130 cases, only one more member was a deputy in the Republican Dáil. No civil servants served in the pre-Free State body.

The two most important organisations in relation to nationalist aspirations are the Gaelic League and the Gaelic Athletic Association (G.A.A.). Of the 109 elected members of the political elite, with 10 missing cases in each category 35 (35 per cent) of the members belonged to the G.A.A. Forty (40 per cent) belonged to the Gaelic League. When increasing the number of members to 194 (and taking into account 28 missing cases), the G.A.A. claimed 42 (25 per cent) members with only 4 civil servants. A total of 59 (36 per cent) belonged to the Gaelic League, with 10 being civil servants. This larger number of members in the Gaelic League in the civil service reflects the traditionally heavy influence of the language enthusiasts in the Department of Education.

In the entire membership of the political elite, only 12 (6 per cent) served in the Irish army. Among the 109 elected members, this number is 10 (9 per cent). Most of this service may be accounted for by the newer members of the political elite who served during the emergency years between 1939 and 1945. Army service is simply not a prerequisite to higher office.

Family Ties

In Ireland family relationships are most important. Family size tends to be large, and family members, even cousins, have contact with one another. It is not unlikely, therefore, that these contacts should be used for political benefit as well as being instrumental in socialisation. Thus, this Irish characteristic is carried into the Dáil and Senate with relatively large numbers of individuals having relations in both houses. Working with the Dáil in 1961 and 1965, John Whyte found that in the first, 23 per cent of the deputies were related to some former or already sitting deputy. In 1965, this figure had increased to 28 per cent.[4] In this study, the question was asked whether the members of the political elite had any relations in either the Dáil or the Senate.

Among the 109 elected members, 35 (32 per cent) were related to someone in the Dáil or Senate. This figure is slightly higher than the Whyte study but may be explained by the inclusion of the Senate which the Whyte study eliminates. When the number of cases is increased to 130, the number of those with relations increases by one and drops to 28 per cent.

Although the inherited seat supposedly figures prominently in the process of gaining office, it is not widespread among the members of the political elite. In this work, the inherited seat refers to immediate succession of a son, nephew, or widow to a seat held by a father, uncle, or husband. Among the 109 cases, 7 (6 per cent) inherited seats. When the number was increased to 130, no addition to the number of inherited seats was found. More important than immediate inheritance of a seat may be the utilisation of a respected family name in a later attempt for political status. The number of individuals who have been related to someone in the political elite is considerably smaller than in the case of those related to individuals in the Dáil and Senate. A total of 15 (14 per cent)

41

of the 109 cases had relations in the political elite. With the addition of the 21 others, that number was increased to 16. Among the 64 civil servants, 3 had relations in the political elite. Two of these individuals—Maurice and John Moynihan —were brothers who served as secretaries of the Department of the Taoiseach, an appointment which may have had more of a political connotation than it does now.

It would seem that the Irish political elite is one which is largely professional and more highly educated than the general population. The elected elite is fairly evenly divided in terms of revolutionary participants or non-participants, urban-rural differences, and membership in the nationalist organisations. Sharp differences were found between the elected members of the elite and the civil servants, but this was expected given the non-political role of the civil service. Differences between the revolutionary and post-revolutionary groups and the urban and rural members of the elite will be examined in the next two chapters.

NOTES

[1]T. W. Freeman, *Ireland: A General and Regional Geography,* London 1965, 146-51.

[2]See *Investment in Education,* report of the Survey Team appointed by the Minister for Education in October 1962, Dublin, published by the Stationery Office, p. 4.

[3]Terence de Vere White, 'Social Life in Ireland, 1927-37' in *Years of the Great Test 1926-39,* ed. by Francis MacManus, The Thomas Davis Lectures, Cork 1967, 24.

[4]See John Whyte, *Dáil Deputies,* Dublin: Tuairim Pamphlet.

4

Social Class and Other Differences between Revolutionary and Post-Revolutionary Elites

Earlier it was suggested that one can discern a greater pragmatism in the contemporary elite at least insofar as its approach to economic matters is concerned. The shift from revolutionary to post-revolutionary environment is thought to be the major factor in explaining differences between earlier and later elite groups. Those who participated in the revolutionary era were cultural as well as political nationalists and set goals that were based upon their particular perceptions of what an Irish Ireland should be. The members of the political elite today have not been through the revolutionary experience—most were not born at the time. In brief, although no doubt subject to graphic descriptions of the period as children, these younger members of the elite have not shared the same intense experience as actual participants.

The question that must be asked in this chapter is whether any substantial differences may be found between the revolutionary and post-revolutionary groups. Whether the shift to a pragmatic orientation may be explained solely by reference to the experience of the revolution giving way to a less harrowing socialisation process is not entirely clear. This chapter, then, is concerned with other possible differences between the revolutionary and post-revolutionary elite. Specifically, the chapter focuses on possible differences in areas of marginality, urban-rural background, and social class differences. Marginality refers to whether the individual comes from the major social formations in the society or whether he comes from groups that are outside the mainstream of that particular community.

Why men decide to participate in a revolt against the existing authority in the state is an open question. To the Marxist theorists, revolution is an endemic condition in society. Given the existence of one class always oppressing another class it is no wonder that societies may be said to be characterised by the potential for violence. History progresses from one epoch to the next through revolution. For the non-Marxist sociologist and political scientist, the revolutionary act is more difficult to explain. If one looks at a society in terms of a community of shared values, how then can one come to grips with the situation in which a segment of that community has taken up arms against it? This is especially pertinent when considering the role of the leader in the revolutionary situation. Can the revolutionary elite be identified as having qualities that are different from the general masses of the population?

In studying the backgrounds of large numbers of revolutionary elites some political scientists have suggested that these individuals may be described as marginal. Moskos, in paraphrasing Lasswell *et al.*, suggests 'that an initial radical revolutionary elite is characterised by a membership which is intellectual, Western exposed, and marginal in its ethnicity, and that the second generation of the radical revolutionary elite witnesses a rise in heartland born, less educated and non-Western exposed individuals'.[1] This, of course, has greater relevance to the developing systems of Africa and Asia in which the largest number of revolutionary leaders tended to be well-educated, in marked contrast to the rest of the population, and, very frequently, extremely well-travelled because of education outside of the country. One of the background features that would be examined while studying the elites of one of the developing systems would be the travel experiences of members of that elite group, as well as where those individuals were educated.

Lerner, in his study of the early Nazi elite in Germany,[2] looked at the problem of marginality by classifying the back-

44

ground characteristics of those who had served in government prior to the Nazi seizure of power, and then suggested that people who had characteristics different from those who served earlier must be considered marginal. He found that the early members of the Nazi elite did, in fact, display marginal characteristics. In his study of the Albanian elite, Moskos suggested :

> Persons may be marginal when they belong to distinct and minority religious groups. In a rural and isolated society, ethnic groups with relatively greater exposure to the world community tend to be marginal. In a society largely illiterate, advanced education can be a marginal trait.[3]

What both Lerner and Moskos are telling us is that one may determine marginality only in terms of the particular community that one is studying. A person is marginal when he has certain characteristics that set him apart from the vast majority of individuals in that community. The new elite may be considered marginal if it displays markedly different characteristics from the group preceding it.

Surely this concept is punctuated by a great many problems. By the breadth of the concept virtually any member of the community must be considered a marginal man in certain respects. The person with blue eyes and blonde hair in the brown-eyed black-haired community is marginal. Further, there exists a compulsion to call someone marginal because he is a revolutionary. But if the concept is to be useful the person must be marginal in terms of the majority community prior to his becoming revolutionary. Thus we would have to say that Hitler was a marginal man because he was Austrian, Catholic, without a university education, and petit bourgeois at a time when national leaders were Prussian, Protestant, educated, and decidedly upper class and upper middle class. Eamon de Valera was marginal because he was born abroad and only half-Irish in his background. They were not marginal because they were revolutionaries; rather, their marginality preceded their revolutionary behaviour. Whether marginality is a cause of revolutionary behaviour is another question. But it may be said that one examines marginality because those who do not fit the picture of the average man in the community may well be less affected by the prevailing values of that community.

Marginality in Ireland may be determined by first examining what the majority of the people happen to be. A critical selection of significant variables should establish whether or not a high proportion of the members of the political elite do or do not display these characteristics. Hence, membership of a Protestant Church would have to be considered marginal in Ireland with the overwhelming majority of people in the state being Catholic. Since most people living in Ireland were born within the country—far more have left with heavy emigration than have come in—then birth outside of Ireland could be considered marginal. Additionally, because most people living in the Republic were not born in the North, if a member of the political elite did come from a Northern county then he could be considered marginal. As noted in Chapter 3 very few members of the political elite are from the North. Are members of the political elite who come from the North in the revolutionary or post-revolutionary category? Further, the border counties in the Republic are somewhat different from the remainder of Ireland in that (a) there is a heavier concentration of Protestants in each of these counties and (b) the socialisation process may be somewhat different since the physical presence of the border may have some effect on the outlooks of people from that region. Thus, for present purposes, we will consider birth in a border region a condition of marginality.

In fact, the revolutionary elite was found to be somewhat marginal in terms of the criteria that have been suggested above. If we include all 32 counties, six members of the political elite were born outside the country. Four of these were revolutionary participants. The other two who were born outside of Ireland, Seán MacBride and Erskine Childers, were the sons of revolutionary heroes. MacBride was the son of John MacBride, one of the martyred leaders of the 1916 Rising. Childers is the son of one of the chief propagandists during the revolutionary and Civil War period. The elder Childers was executed by the Free State forces as a republican during the Civil War. To add to this example of marginality, he was also born and educated outside of Ireland and is a Protestant as well. Eamon de Valera, who is easily the most important of the revolutionary figures to have survived that period, was born in the United States of an Irish mother and Spanish father. While it is true that he was brought to Ireland during very early childhood, the fact that he was an American citizen at the time of the Rising probably saved him from execution in 1916. Additionally, this fact of his having been brought back to Ireland at an early age may well have contributed to a sense of mission that he had in becoming a revolutionary. While it is certainly beyond the scope of this work to comment on the psychological state of one, or any, of the revolutionary figures, marginality must be responsible for the individual's having a revolutionary mission. Some very significant political biographies have commented on the types of variables that may have been instrumental in attitude formation.[4]

All individuals who have served in the political elite and who were born in one of the northern six counties were revolutionary participants—although in one case it was not necessarily as a willing activist. Eoin MacNeill was the founder of the Gaelic League and the Volunteers and served as a member of the Cumann na nGaedheal government until the problems of the Boundary Commission dispute in 1925. Seán MacEntee, who retired from public life in 1969, was a participant in the Easter Rising and one of the earliest members of Fianna Fáil. Frank Aiken, who was the head of the Irish Republican Army during the closing days of the Civil War, served in various capacities in Fianna Fáil governments since 1932. He was, as a matter of fact, the last of the revolutionary figures to give up elite status in 1969 when he retired as Minister for External Affairs. Ernest Blythe, who has had a distinguished career in a non-political capacity, was a revolutionary activist and a very devoted believer in the language movement. In addition, Blythe, who taught Irish to fellow prisoners in the days after Easter, 1916, is a Protestant. Joseph Connolly is a rather interesting figure of this period. He was one of the few members of the government to have served in a ministerial capacity while a member of the Senate. He never served in the Dáil. When he left his post, he went into the civil service as Chairman of the Board of Public Works. No other former minister made the transition to the civil service. The somewhat unwilling revolutionary participant was Patrick McGilligan who served during the Cosgrave administration and also served in governments until 1957. Although sympathetic to the revolutionary cause, he did not take an active part in the revolution but was arrested anyway. He was released quickly when it was determined by the authorities that he was not engaged in action designed to eject the British.

Earlier it was suggested that partition has been more thorough than later governments would care to admit. The fact that no contemporary member of the political elite was born in the North is but another indication of the growing localism and actual separation from the North. Additionally, to refer to birth in the North as being a marginal quality is questionable when considering that at the time these men joined in revolutionary activity—in fact, first took an interest in revolutionary activity and cultural nationalism—Ireland had not yet been partitioned. Nevertheless, coming from areas that were largely Protestant and not particularly hotbeds of rebellion, it must be considered a somewhat marginal characteristic.

Of those who were born in border counties—each of which has a higher proportion of Protestants than any other county in the Republic—none is a Protestant. One of the best known of those individuals who have served as members of the political elite is Neil Blaney, the former Minister for Agriculture in the Lynch administration. Blaney is a son of a revolutionary and Civil War activist who also served in the Dáil, prior to the junior Blaney's entering that body. The young Blaney has been one of the most outspoken of the post-revolutionary elite with regard to the role that the government

48

of the Republic should play in the difficult Northern situation. This may be the result of the proximity of Donegal, his home county, to the North. None of the other individuals within this group had been distinguished publicly by any activity involving the question of partition prior to 1969. Thus it may be concluded that, given the clear lack of difference between the revolutionary and post-revolutionary elites insofar as coming from a border county is concerned, birth in this area may not be looked upon as being marginal.

The early Irish political elite may have been slightly marginal in terms of the kind of background characteristics that punctuated both earlier and later elite groups. The characteristics of the members of the revolutionary elite indicate that a slight tendency exists to come from outside of what might be considered as the heartland of the Irish system. But when compared to some other revolutionary elite groups, the Irish revolutionary figures do not display particularly strong marginal characteristics, and it would certainly be stretching a concept to suggest vast differences on this point between the revolutionary and post-revolutionary elite.

Urban-rural differences

Ireland is variously referred to as a rural or a non-urbanised society. Of course, this is changing with a continually higher proportion of people living in villages or towns of over 1,500 with each census. The specific question asked was whether members of the political elite who participated in the revolution were more likely to have come from urban backgrounds than those who did not take part in the revolution. A more urban background for revolutionaries is a reasonable expectation. The kind of environment that the urban area provides may conceivably be considered more efficacious for revolutionary activity. Certainly the major revolutionary activity in western states has tended to be urban based. Whether the revolutionaries are from these urban places is another question.

With regard to the size of the city in which the member of the elite was born and/or raised, two questions were asked.

49

The first question dealt with the members of the elite who came from a town or city with a population in excess of 1,500. No significant difference was found between the revolutionary and post-revolutionary groups. A second question dealt with any differences that existed between the two groups with regard to the size of the city from which the individuals may have come. Here, too, in the more specific breakdown no real difference was found between the two groups.

While these findings indicate that there would seem to be no relationship between the more pragmatic approach to political problems that characterises the contemporary elite, and rural (or urban) background, no attempt is made here to suggest that those who participated in the revolution tended to be more urban than the general population. Certainly a number of the great revolutionary leaders were urban-born and raised—Griffith and O'Kelly were among them. But men such as Collins and de Valera were rural-born and raised. It may be suggested, however, that the first introduction to the revolutionary experience came in the urban environment, not the rural one.

A study of this kind indicates how little we really know from a sociological standpoint about the composition of revolutionary movements, the general socialisation process which has been experienced by the revolutionary figure, and, with regard to Ireland specifically, what the actual factors were that influenced so many individuals to risk and give their lives. We know generally how important was the impact of the new cultural nationalism, but the jump from cultural nationalism to revolutionary participation is very difficult to explain.

Social Class Differences

Whether revolutionaries come from different social class backgrounds than do post-revolutionaries is an open question. Surely the researcher examining the backgrounds of the leaders of the Russian revolutionary Bolsheviks must be disappointed to learn of the non-working-class origins of a large number of these individuals. But much is obscure when

50

examining the social class origins of many of the revolutionary participants in Ireland who later became members of the political elite. It is not much more satisfactory when trying to determine the social class backgrounds of members of the contemporary political elite group.

The major problem here is a critical lack of information. In attempting to determine the social class of an individual, ideally it is useful to be able to learn as much as possible about the parents of that individual. One would need information—at least with regard to the father—concerning education, occupation and, of course, any titles that the individual might have. The fact that so little information is available concerning the fathers of members of the political elite is indicative of (a) a poor method of keeping records or (b) social class background that is not particularly high. In this case, it may be assumed that few members of the political elite have come from social class backgrounds that could be considered high. A fairly large number would be considered lower middle class and agricultural, from what we know of the background of the parents. This refers both to the revolutionary and post-revolutionary members of the elite.

To determine if there was a difference in social class between the revolutionary and post-revolutionary groups, an attempt was made to examine the types of education received. Here we are dealing essentially with the level of education attained. Except for one level—attendance at a university—the revolutionary and post-revolutionary groups are not different.

With regard to university attendance, there are several factors which might be considered which would explain the higher attendance at a university among members of the contemporary elite and none of these reflects social class differences. First, more people have been attending university than was the case at one time. If we were to examine the general attendance figures for the entire population we would, no doubt, find an increase in the number of individuals attending a university. Second, many of the individuals who participated in the revolution began this activity at a rather early age. In the period in which they might have attended a university they may have been fighting or detained by the British. In any event, the slight difference between the two groups does not seem indicative of class distinction. Rather, what it does seem to indicate is the coming to age in different periods of time.

Another area in which the social class differences could be determined is in an examination of the practised occupations of the members of both groups. Earlier, the various occupational categories were listed and, in composing the categories with reference to differences between the revolutionary and post-revolutionary elite, there are some differences in three of the categories. The three categories in which differences may be determined are those that include the labour-union, journalistic-artistic, and the managerial occupations. Additionally, a slight difference is found in the civil service category (among members of the elite whose status is not determined by high civil service position). Among members of the revolutionary group, a number of individuals, including Michael Collins, had entered the British civil service at rather early ages. Once the war for independence began, they left these positions. The civil service experience served them well, for when an alternative service was established to rival the British bureaucracy the revolutionary group was quite successful.

With regard to those who fit into the labour category—which includes individuals who have served as labour union officials—all represent a post-revolutionary background. But it should be remembered that the immediate pre-1969 Labour shadow cabinet was included within the elite group. With the inclusion of this group several union officials were brought into the elite category. If these Labour members were eliminated from elite status, then there are fewer labour union officials, all in the post-revolutionary group. It should be understood that the Labour party in the Republic has not been a large group, and with partition, a potential Labour constituency in the North was eliminated.

52

Five members of the contemporary elite group may be considered part of the managerial class. This compares with only one member of the revolutionary group. This, however, may be a bit confusing. A rather large number of revolutionary figures including Seán Lemass and James Ryan have served in managerial capacity. This, however, tended to occur after the individual had been successful in a political career. The contemporary members of the elite tended to begin their careers in business, achieve managerial status and then enter political life, a considerably different career route than the revolutionary figure who achieved fame in a political career and then retired from public life to reap the rewards of his fame.

Differences were found in the category which includes the occupations of journalism and art. In this category, Ireland follows a pattern that has occurred in other post-revolutionary societies. Revolutionary participants tended to practise journalistic occupations in propagandist capacities. Pre-eminent among the journalist-propagandists was Arthur Griffith but the category also includes Seán T. O'Kelly, Patrick Little, Desmond FitzGerald and Ernest Blythe. They were involved in the publication of certain nationalist journals which supported anything from the moderately soft home rule proposals made by Arthur Griffith (and his concept of a dual monarchy) to the more militantly republican ideal of total separation from Great Britain. The members of the post-revolutionary elite group are noticeably lacking in these occupational categories.

Summarily, with the exceptions mentioned above, no real differences were determined between revolutionary and post-revolutionary elite groups with regard to occupations. The difference found in the journalistic-artistic category was not unexpected. In fact, had it not occurred, then Ireland would have been able to claim at least one area of uniqueness when compared to other revolutionary and post-revolutionary societies. Revolutions produce propagandists.

Once again, some caution must be exercised in the interpretation of these findings. What little data are available deal only with members of the political elite. One could argue that the Irish revolution was indeed a class struggle—oppressed class against the oppressor class. But in terms of the two elite groups, the first being comprised of revolutionary participants and the second of those who did not participate in the revolution, no real class differences were determined. Thus, with special reference to the political elite, the shift from strong support for cultural nationalism to a pragmatic stand on most, especially economic, issues does not seem to be the result of a shift in class background.

In fact, there would seem to be very little difference between the two groups in any of the background characteristics with the exception of (1) having participated or not participated in the revolutionary era and (2) the career patterns. How the career patterns varied between the two groups is considered in the next chapter.

NOTES

[1]Charles Moskos, 'From Monarchy to Communism: The Social Transformation of the Albanian Elite' in *Social Change in Developing Areas,* ed. by Herbert R. Barringer, George Blanksten and Raymond W. Mack, Cambridge, Mass. 1963, 215.

[2]Daniel Lerner, *World Revolutionary Elites,* ed. by Harold Lasswell and Daniel Lerner, Boston 1966, 194-318.

[3]Moskos, *op. cit.,* 214.

[4]See Lewis Edinger, *Kurt Schumacher: A Study in Personality and Political Behavior,* Stanford 1965.

5

Recruitment into the Political Elite

How do people come to elite positions or status? One
approach is to examine the regular patterns of career development exhibited by members of the elite. Where a significant
number demonstrate the same career attribute (e.g. political
positions held, party service, organisation affiliations), it is
reasonable to accept this as characteristic of a particular
group or groups within the elite. Once the career patterns
have been established, it is important to discover why these
patterns exist and what factors might explain different career
types. Do, for example, different career patterns exist in
different time periods? If in the same period of time several
career patterns exist, what factors explain these differences?
Are urban and rural career types different from one another?
Finally, if only one pattern is available in a particular time
period, what reason may be found to explain the lack of
alternative routes to high position?

The study of political career patterns as part of the area of
political elite recruitment has a vital place in the literature.
Lester Seligman, in a study dealing with the Israeli political
elite, has suggested the importance of political elite recruitment for two reasons:

The elite recruitment both reflects and affects the society.
As a dependent variable, it expresses the value system of
the society and its degree of consistency and contradiction,
the degree and type of representativeness of the system, the
basis of social stratification and its articulation with the
political system, and the structure and change in political
roles. As a factor which affects change or as an independent
variable, elite recruitment patterns determine avenues for
political participation and status, influence the kind of
policies that will be enacted, accelerate or retard changes,

55

E

effect the distribution of status and prestige, and influence the stability of the system.[1]

Thus, the study of political careers, or political recruitment, allows us to study two separate areas. First, through the study of the career routes, system values may be examined more carefully. What service does the community expect from its political leaders as these leaders are climbing higher toward elite status? Second, career routes may help to explain attitudes of members of the elite and policies adopted by the governments. While several studies have dealt with this problem, this work is concerned with the first point. A third point is raised by Seligman, specifically with regard to political parties. He states, 'The critical contribution of political parties to leadership is their strategic role in the structure of political opportunity. The latter refers to the various chances offered members of social strata to enter and compete for specific roles.'[2] We may expand this point. It is not only the political party which provides an opportunity structure, but other parts of the political and social structures as well which provide this framework of opportunity. Thus, this study of career types provides insights into the perceptions of individual members of the political elite regarding what constitutes the optimal route(s) to elite status. Simply asked, how does the aspiring politician choose a particular route to office?

We have no firm evidence to indicate that the individual beginning a political career in Ireland chooses certain paths of least resistance. Careful analysis of the political career patterns does, however, indicate enough regularity to suggest that the young, ambitious politician has very clear ideas concerning his political possibilities.

Dealing with the opportunity structure and the perceptions of those who reach high position, Joseph Schlesinger has constructed what he terms an ambition theory. 'The central assumption of ambition theory . . . is that politicians respond to their office goals. The theory assumes, in other words, that politicians act in the manner which they consider appropriate to the achievement of office.'[3] In this approach, Schlesinger relies heavily on Anthony Downs and the latter's definition of the 'rational man', or 'a man who moves toward his goals in a way which, to the best of his knowledge, uses the least possible input of scarce resources per unit of valued output'.[4]

As a study of opportunity structure and career routes the Schlesinger work is quite interesting. While he utilises background information concerning the career attributes of a wide variety of office holders, he does not really determine if the politician in question followed a clear plan to reach high office. Nevertheless, the determination of these routes does tell what paths are most likely to be followed, and from this it is fair to assume that the politician with intimate knowledge of the operation of the political system, as well as the problems that arise in his own constituency, is aware not only of what route is most suitable, but what is perhaps the only route given the particular limitations of the system and the political structures. It would be a very foolish young politician indeed who could not perceive a suitable path to high office.

In Ireland, two clearly defined career types were determined. They were found through the use of factor analysis, a technique which allows the researcher to determine empirically clusters of variables that are inter-related with one another. The two career patterns in evidence were the early revolutionary career type and what may be defined as the contemporary career type. Within the contemporary type are two further patterns, the urban and rural elite type. What distinguishes the contemporary elite pattern from the revolutionary pattern is the greater localism that exists today and the very clearly defined stepping-stone pattern. In this section we deal with only 109 elected members of the elite, those who have served in the governments. The civil service career pattern has not altered, indicating the high degree of stability in the Irish bureaucracy since, and indeed before, the founding of the state.

The Revolutionary Elite

The lack of any connection between the pre-revolutionary elite, i.e. the members of the Irish parliamentary party, and the revolutionary elite is demonstrated by the dearth of individuals in the revolutionary elite who had served in the parliamentary group. As F. S. L. Lyons has stated, 'the blow to the Irish Party (Parliamentary Party) received in 1916 was not far short of mortal'.[5] Following the Easter Rising, the discredited parliamentary group was virtually eliminated in elections in which leaders and participants in the revolutionary movement—members of the Sinn Féin organisation —were elected to parliamentary seats. In the general election of 1918 the members of the parliamentary party were able to hold only 6 seats while Sinn Féin swept 73. Refusing to be seated in the British parliament, Dáil Eireann was founded and began functioning as the government of the Irish Republic.

Several features distinguish between the career patterns of the revolutionary and non-revolutionary elite in Ireland. Obviously, the socialisation experiences were considerably different. First, one group participated in the revolutionary war and Civil War as well, and its members belonged to certain nationalist organisations. This might seem rather a trite point, but in fact it is critical to an understanding of the changing goals of the Irish political elite. While treated in other studies,[6] it was the revolutionary dominated elite groups that found strong cultural commitments and the post-revolutionary groups that have demonstrated a decidedly pragmatic and economics-oriented style. This has not been a subtle difference. It has often been suggested that contemporary members of Fianna Fáil have more in common with members of Fine Gael and Labour than they do with their predecessors in Fianna Fáil.[7] Second, the revolutionary participants represented a 'national' rather than local constituency. A far greater number of revolutionary participants were adopted by constituencies other than those in which they were born or lived than are today. Additionally, many early elite members (a) were adopted for multiple constituencies and (b) changed constituencies. In fact, localism is quite clearly one of the most significant features of the Irish political system. Members of the revolutionary elite were thrust into a national role without having gone through the progression of local offices that is demanded of the contemporary political elite.

The first characteristic of the revolutionary elite was its youthfulness. This concept of youthfulness was modified somewhat by the discussion in Chapter 3. Youthfulness is discussed here because it has relevance to the fact that the members of the revolutionary elite tended to enter the national political scene at such an early age that they hadn't the time to have participated in local politics. In his study of the Albanian political elite, Moskos has suggested these reasons why youthfulness is functional for elite co-operation and cohesion. First, he says, youthfulness permits the elite to remain relatively free from physical incapacity during its period of service. Second, since the members of the elite come to power at a young age, it is highly unlikely that any participated in the regime that is being displaced. And third, the common experiences of the revolution may aid in the elimination of any dissension once independence is achieved.[8] Moskos' first and third points will be discussed in the conclusion. But the second point which deals with the lack of formal ties with the previous political leaders must be stressed. The revolutionary elite type is characterised by its lack of connection with any of the formal governing apparatus that came before.

Members of the revolutionary elite had considerably different organisational commitments than do the members of the contemporary elite. Most significant of the organisations was the Gaelic League. It helped to create a concept of cultural nationalism that had been lacking in the earlier home rule movement. The Gaelic League acted as a magnet to the young nationalists interested in Ireland as a separate entity from the British. Patrick Pearse was a member of the Gaelic League as were the two charismatic leaders of the revolution, Michael Collins and Eamon de Valera.

It is worth noting that Gaelic League membership tended to precede revolutionary activity. Although the founders of the League disavowed the political trends that eventually

59

affected it, it became perhaps the chief socialising agent in the development of nationalist tendencies. While the continued existence of the Irish language may well be the result of Gaelic League activity, the most important by-product of the League may well have been the production of a generation of nationalists willing to fight for Ireland's independence.

An attempt was made to determine whether the organisation has declined in membership over the years but no figures were available from the League. It is obvious, however, that membership has declined. It certainly has among members of the political elite. Among members of the revolutionary elite, some 69 per cent belonged at one time to the Gaelic League. This figure stands at 15 per cent for members of the contemporary group. Reasons for the decline might be twofold : (1) the language issue is not as important as it was since it is taught in the schools, and, at least officially, its decline has been averted, and (2) the independence of Ireland is a reality and the League is, therefore, no longer necessary functionally. Additionally, other more vigorous Irish language movements have replaced the earlier hegemony of the League.

The Gaelic Athletic Association (G.A.A.), which was founded in much the same circumstances as the Gaelic League, has retained its hold on much of the youth since the revolutionary period. No real difference was found in membership figures in the organisation between the revolutionary and post-revolutionary figures. Later it will be suggested that the difference that could be found in the G.A.A. membership is that between urban and rural members of the political elite. The G.A.A. does seem a vital agency in the rural areas for political contacts. While the Gaelic League has declined over the years for a variety of reasons, not the least of which has been the government co-optation of the language movement, the G.A.A. has managed to keep the young people interested. This continued interest has not come without modification of G.A.A. standards, however, as the ban on foreign games has finally been lifted.

A lack of local orientation is one of the more outstanding characteristics of the revolutionary elite. A generally lower level of active participation than the non-revolutionary elite at the local level prior to service in the national political scene was evident in this early group. No real difference was found with regard to membership on urban district councils. A number of early leaders, for example, had served on the Dublin Corporation council prior to the revolution. But insofar as membership of a county council or representation in the Dáil of the constituency in which the individual was born and/or raised, was concerned, the revolutionary figure is much lower on the scale.

Service on a county council was not vital to membership in the political elite for revolutionary figures. However, this feature is more noticeably a characteristic of the later elite. In fact, only 29 per cent of the revolutionary elite served on a county council while 51 per cent of the contemporary group have.

The lack of a strong local orientation among members of the revolutionary elite is reinforced, albeit not to a very significant degree, by the growing number of members of the elite who represent their home districts in the Dáil. Some 70 per cent of the revolutionary group represented the home district while among the post-revolutionary group it is 84 per cent. This does not seem a tremendous difference—and statistically it is not; however, taken with the much smaller county council associations of the revolutionary elite, it does point to a more national group.

Thus, the picture of the composite careers of the members of the revolutionary elite which emerges is composed of the following components: (1) participation in the revolutionary struggle and, possibly, the Civil War as well, (2) adoption by a constituency for a seat in the Dáil, with a fairly high proportion having been elected to a seat in Westminster, and (3) eventual ministerial status. Added to this is the very high degree of active support for the Gaelic League, to which most of the members of the revolutionary group belonged.

61

As indicated, the members of the contemporary elite group are more strongly typified by this localism and step-by-step progression to high office. Within this group some difference was determined between those who come from urban areas and those from the rural areas. Additionally, one major difference is to be found between the members of Fianna Fáil and the other parties. But this is the result of Fianna Fáil's almost uninterrupted control of office since 1932. It is suggested in this work that a 'normalisation' process is occurring in Irish politics. Localism, a clear feature of the Irish tradition of kinship, is re-asserting itself now that the revolutionary era is becoming a distant memory. As this period dies, the new era is typified by the day to day work that the politician must do in order to retain his following. This is the kind of work that the local man, with his intimate knowledge of the people and general features of his constituency, can do more successfully than the 'drafted' candidate who might well be liked by the party's national executive, but not by the local organisation.

A first step on the route to elite status is service on a county council or urban district council. The difference here is determined by whether the individual is from an urban or a rural area, although it should be stated that 18 members of the political elite have served on both an urban and a county council at one time. Eleven individuals served only on the urban bodies while 24 served on county bodies. The difference is significant enough to suggest that urban and rural members of the political elite begin their careers in politics from different starting points which are determined by the particular political structure of their local community.

Both the urban and county councils are reasonably important in the operation of local government. Formally, at least, county councils are active in five areas: roads, public assistance, health services, sanitary services, and housing. These areas, it should be noted, are ones in which the possibilities of patronage might seem very real indeed. The placing of men on road crews, for example, is a local prerogative. Chubb states, 'As is the case at national level with T.D.s, the elected member is a consumer representative and more of a factor in the administration of services than a policy maker or legislator.'[9] This, of course, is limited by the highly professionalised civil service which has such strong authority even in the political activities of the state at the local level. Thus, the opportunities for patronage are limited by the system rules.

But, strictly speaking, these services are not of particular interest to this study. It is to a different function that we must look in order to understand the importance of the local body as a part of the career pattern of members of the Irish political elite. The county councils and urban district councils serve as a training ground for the future political leader. Additionally, they provide a way for the party to reward the individual who has given long years of service with a place of honour in his 'old age'. But for the younger politician, membership on a local body provides a place where he may give speeches, appear to influence decisions, and meet some of the local influentials while he is waiting for the local T.D. to die, retire, or make some catastrophic blunder. Essentially it is a place where the individual may either (a) retire gracefully or (b) begin his trek to greener pastures—membership in the Dáil representing the eventual end. No payment is received by the member of the county council. Thus, unless he is a particularly altruistic individual, such service must provide other rewards.

With each county council having between 21 and 31 seats (County Cork being the exception with 46 seats) the county councils provide a much greater opportunity structure for the ambitious politician than early membership in the Dáil (which has only 144 seats). There exists a greater possibility that the newcomer to politics will have a chance to obtain a seat. As a matter of fact once an individual goes into the Dáil and even into an elite position, he is very likely to remain in the county or urban council because of the continued local contacts these bodies provide for him. When interviewed, several individuals complained about the amount of time that had to be given to local business. Yet they were not keen to have legislation which would prohibit service on a local body while in the Dáil. Such legislation would eliminate one of the more effective methods of contact with constituents. Thus, for a first step toward elite status, the political structures as well as the tradition of localism define the direction that one must take.

Another traditional avenue in the rural areas is membership in the G.A.A. This might seem a particularly unimportant step toward eliteness because it is obviously not an organisation that has tremendous influence on the government decision-area. While it is not particularly important from that standpoint, functionally it is an organisation that might be vital to the future success of the young politician. It is an organisation through which the rural politician may come to know many of the locally important people. In rural Ireland—much like other societies in which there are only a limited number of heroes to spare—the voters are pleased if their candidates are G.A.A. men. Athletic prowess has traditionally been a method of public exposure. Surely someone such as Mr Lynch, the Taoiseach, was not hurt by his athletic fame. One should bear in mind that despite the fact that the G.A.A. is a national organisation, it is in the rural areas that this particular body serves as a means to elite status.

While the Gaelic League is not a particularly important organisation today, where members of the contemporary elite group do tend to belong is in the rural areas as well. This might suggest the closer ties to the traditional values that might be found in the countryside. It should be clear, however, that the Gaelic League cannot really be considered a part of the career pattern of the contemporary political elite.

By the time the young politician has developed a local reputation of sorts through service on an urban or county council and, if a rural-based person, work in the G.A.A., he is in a position to seek a higher office, which, in the Irish political system, is a seat in the Dáil. Chubb has stated :

On the whole, it is the record of service of the party nominees that electors look for, and the local councillor aspiring to a seat in the Dáil knows this well and acts accordingly. If he gets a seat, he knows that the surest way to retain it is by continuing that service which, indeed, due to his greater eminence and wider contacts, he is now able to improve and widen.[10]

Once again, it is a combination of system values and political structures that defines both the steps that the individual takes to get to the Dáil and the role that he will play once he is there. The political structure defines the steps because Dáil membership is virtually the only path to ministerial, i.e. elite, position. Party structure, the selection of candidates at the local level, and the complicated Irish electoral system make it imperative that the T.D. continue his brokerage role if he expects to remain in office. It is obvious that it is here that the T.D.s greatest strength lies. Bax has suggested that at the outset of the Irish Free State with its Civil War it was

> possible for politicians to be elected on the basis of their attitudes toward this issue. Now that this issue is dying out and new ones are lacking, it is difficult for them to attract a following on a 'moral' basis. Under the present circumstances in Ireland the electoral system not only provides new opportunities for politicians, it also forces them to play another role to attract voters, namely the role of broker.[11]

Simply put, the constituents tend to see the T.D. as fulfilling his job if it appears that he is getting personal favours for them.

This dependence upon the T.D. is the result partly of system values. Here we are on very speculative grounds, for the type of survey research which might provide some insights into how the average individual views his government is woefully lacking. This is unfortunate as it would provide the social scientist with a most interesting area of study. Chubb has suggested that 'oligarchic rule, underemployment and poverty all led most Irish people to view government, even though it was alien, as a potential source of help, jobs or favours, provided one knew how to tap it'.[12] Whether this description is accurate, the T.D. was, and is, perceived as that individual with the ability to act as the middle man. Most significantly, from the comparative standpoint, the Irish politician has carried this attitude with him when he has emigrated. American city machines certainly followed this pattern. It would be quite interesting to examine political arrangements in British cities with large Irish populations. Very similar patterns could emerge despite the somewhat different British political system.

The success that a T.D. has as a local agent must continue even after he has made the successful jump from T.D. to Minister. The fact that he has achieved elite status is no reason for him to minimise his local contacts. One of the reasons that some of the revolutionary figures had such poor re-election records toward the end of their careers was the lack of local connection. Despite the years of national service, local constituents came to feel that they had been neglected. For the post-revolutionary members of the political elite this is a very clear lesson indeed. Consequently, ministers and parliamentary secretaries do not neglect their constituency ties. This may mean dealing with more than 100 representations a week from constituents both in Dublin and at home. They must grow weary of such contact, but lack of accessibility will damage chances for their re-election.

A brief word needs to be said about the Senate. The ambitious young politician may be defeated his first time round. If the party sees the individual as having a useful political future, then the Senate is an ideal place to await further opportunities for as Coogan so aptly tells us, the Senate 'tends to be a place wherein, to parody the catechism definition of purgatory, some souls suffer for a time before they are translated to the Dáil . . .'.[13] The Senate also tends to be the final resting place for the individual who has lost his seat in the Dáil.

While the Senate is not particularly important in the actual passage of legislation—it might be added that given rigid party discipline the Dáil may not be particularly important either—it is not without meaningful political functions. As stated, it is a place of honour for the older politician when he retires from the Dáil or when he loses an election. As in the House of Lords in Great Britain, meaningful debate is still possible with the result being a greater exposure of issues than would occur if debated only in the Dáil. Ministers may still come from the Senate; however, there have been only two in the history of the Irish state. For the purpose of this work, the crucial function of the Senate is its provision of a forum for the young man on his way up. In this way it serves as a potentially significant part of the career pattern.

Once in the Dáil, an element of luck prevails if further success is to be achieved. For members of Fine Gael and Labour the possibility of service in the Shadow Cabinet is important. Should these parties form the government, those who would serve would be largely inexperienced. Fianna Fáil has inadvertently avoided this problem. Through its very long domination of the government it has tended to recruit through use of the position of parliamentary secretary. It is most likely that once an individual serves as a parliamentary secretary he will achieve a ministerial position when a suitable vacancy occurs. It must be borne in mind that this is a particular feature only of the Fianna Fáil career pattern, not of members of other political parties.

Two very clear career patterns are evident in the Irish political elite. The first of these career types is the revolutionary, characterised by its national background. Local ties were not as vital within this group as they appear to be now. This is demonstrated by (1) the substantially lower membership of this group on county councils either prior to or simultaneous with membership in the Dáil and (2) the frequency with which members of the revolutionary elite served in the Dáil as representatives of districts from which they did not come. Further, the members of the revolutionary group tended to belong to the most important of the cultural-nationalist organisations, the Gaelic League. This national orientation is not uncommon in the immediate post-revolutionary system. Those who participated were highly valued by the community and their service was repaid by support in political campaigns. But as the time distance between the revolutionary era and elections grew greater, the opportunity structure altered substantially as other values such as localism became important. Thus, a new elite group grew in which two sub-types may be seen, the urban and rural career patterns. In the first, service on an urban district council is essential prior to election to the Dáil, and in the second, service on a county council seems vital as well as participation in the G.A.A. For both, failure to be elected to the Dáil may be tempered somewhat by appointment to the Senate. Ultimately, however, failure to reach the Dáil ends the possibility of ever attaining elite status. It has also been suggested that a difference results from Fianna Fáil's long service and the other parties' lack of service in government. Fianna Fáil tends to place members of the Dáil in positions as parliamentary secretary prior to the attainment of ministerial status. The other parties, of course, cannot do this. Another factor ought to be kept in mind. No attempt has been made to examine whether the same pattern is to be found among all members of the Dáil. Speculatively, it is suggested that the career patterns for members of the contemporary elite are similar to—or much the same as—those members of the Dáil who have not attained elite status. Among the earlier members of the Dáil—those who did not achieve elite status—it is likely that their career routes are more likely to follow the contemporary pattern of local service. Although it is true that a number of revolutionary heroes and folk-heroes such as Dan Breen served in the Dáil, these men were in the minority and the normalisation process which affected the elite with the passing of the revolutionary generation probably began working on the Dáil somewhat earlier.

NOTES

[1]Lester Seligman, *Leadership in a New Nation*, New York 1964, 7.

[2]Lester Seligman, 'Political Parties and the Recruitment of Political Leaders', in *Political Leadership in Industrialised Societies,* ed. by Lewis Edinger, New York 1967, 294.

[3]Joseph Schlesinger, *Ambition and Politics,* Chicago 1966, 194.

[4]Anthony Downs, *An Economic Theory of Democracy,* New York 1957, 9.

[5]F. S. L. Lyons, 'Dillon, Redmond and the Irish Home Rulers' in *Leaders and Men of the Easter Rising,* ed. by F. X. Martin, London 1967, 39.

[6]See A. S. Cohan, *Revolutionary and Non-Revolutionary Elites: The Irish Political Elite in Transition,* unpublished Ph.D. dissertation, The University of Georgia, Athens, Georgia 1970.

[7]See T. P. Coogan, *Ireland Since the Rising,* London 1966.

[8]Charles Moskos, 'The Social Transformation of the Albanian Elite: The Concept of Elite Generations', paper presented at Northwestern University, Conference on Developing Areas 1961, 17-18.

[9]Basil Chubb, *Government and Politics in Ireland,* London 1970, 287.

[10]Basil Chubb, 'Going about Persecuting Civil Servants: The Role of the Irish Parliamentary Representative', *Political Studies,* XI (1963), 276.

[11]Marten Bax, 'Patronage Irish Style: Irish Politicians as Brokers', unpublished paper, 8.

[12]Basil Chubb, *op. cit.,* 273.

[13]T. P. Coogan, *op. cit.,* 140.

6

Conclusion

What is most striking about the Irish political elite over the past fifty years is the lack of any real change in the social background characteristics of this group since the revolutionary era ended. While we noted in Chapter 4 that the revolutionary elite was somewhat more marginal than the post-revolutionary elite, in general the revolutionary and post-revolutionary elite groups resemble one another in almost all respects.

But Irish society has altered considerably, and that change is reflected in the political elite in at least two ways. First, the goals of the political elite are quite different now. The cultural goals that formed the core of the revolutionary elite's vision of Ireland now have a secondary place. Second, the Irish situation has normalised to the degree that people in any given constituency want a local man to represent them in the Dáil. As a consequence, the career routes of members of the political elite are marked by a greater number of local involvements. The revolutionary figure with few—if any—local contacts is a clear feature of the past. National reputations will be created after attainment of elite status. Prominence on the national scene is unlikely to precede elite status.

In a study of the composition of the 1969 Dáil,[1] Brian Farrell replicated the work done by John Whyte[2] in *Dáil Deputies,* a study completed in 1966, and also considered the work carried out by McCracken.[3] Farrell studied the four routes of entry into the Dáil, which had been suggested earlier by Whyte. These were: (1) 'through participation in the national liberation movement' (2) 'through relationship with former or sitting representatives' (3) 'through local government experience' (4) 'through prominence in sport'. It was noted that time has lessened the significance of the first route, but the second, third and fourth points are thought to be the most important.

A critical point that seems to have been missed—or simply overlooked—by the previously-mentioned works is that the hereditary seat and participation in sport are both aspects of the local connection. What this suggests is that the position taken in this work is correct: that there is but one route to high office, local government experience and a strong local social base. Coming from a political family in Donegal is unlikely to make one a candidate for the Dáil in Wexford or Kerry. G.A.A. ties will enable one to know his local notables. Both of these 'routes' are really supportive of the need for significant local ties. Without these types of ties a really meaningful political career with successful attainment of high office is not likely. While Whyte and Farrell dealt with the Dáil generally, these findings are certainly applicable to the political elite—the elected group —as well.

But this shift from the revolutionary to the post-revolutionary elite has greater ramifications than the alteration of career routes. We have alluded to the reasons for the significance of this shift at the outset of this work. Here we shall reconsider some of the main points in light of the changes in the Irish political elite. Further, some indication of the types of pressures that will bear on the elite will be given.

The change that occurred in Irish society was not without precedent. Kautsky dealt with the shift that takes place in the post-revolutionary society in which the revolutionary elite gives way to the managerial. The Irish situation is a clear example of what Kautsky has in mind. The new men are economically oriented with a view to the establishment of what is considered sound economic policy for steady economic growth. P. Lynch maintains that the revolutionary governments had been dominated by the 'Sinn Féin Myth'. This myth had 'been a decisive influence on public thinking and policy for more than two generations . . . [and had]

71

assumed that Irish political independence implied economic independence'.[4] The 'new men' have not been constrained by such limits.

What has particularly confounded the Irish political scene for so many years was how long the revolutionary elite lingered. In this respect, Ireland has been a unique society. The Soviet revolutionary elite might have lasted were the purges of the 1930s not conducted. Ireland, free from such traumas, was governed by a dominant revolutionary elite group until 1959 when de Valera left active politics. In spite of the presence of the younger men as well as the long service of Lemass who was undoubtedly a pragmatist regardless of his revolutionary service, the revolutionary ethos prevailed until the main figures of that era left active political life. Admittedly, this view could be construed as too simple an interpretation of changes that occurred in Irish political life. The seeds of economic growth may well have been planted earlier; nevertheless, the type of society that Ireland 'ought to become' was seen in different terms by de Valera than by Lemass or Lynch. The rural paradise that de Valera pictured is an image not held by contemporary Irish political leaders.

This brings us back to the three points raised by Moskos with regard to the youthfulness of the revolutionary elite. We have already dealt with the point that members of the revolutionary elite were not likely to have participated in the previous regime. But his two other points are relevant to the conclusion. First, the relative youthfulness of the elite permits it to be free of physical incapacity for a long period. This is most obvious when applied to Ireland. The mortality rate in the revolution and Civil War may have been high, but, since then, the longevity of the Irish revolutionary figures has been nothing short of remarkable. This has added to the other point made by Moskos: the common experiences of the revolution aid in the elimination of dissension once independence is achieved. Consequently, the long-ruling Fianna Fáil group remained relatively unchanged for nearly 30 years.

That lack of dissension is a key consideration in any study of the Irish political elite. Since we determined that, in terms of social composition, the revolutionary experience is the one factor among those that have been considered that separates the revolutionary from post-revolutionary elite, we can suggest that this is also a determining factor in the shift in the goals of the political system. In the work, *Revolutionary Immortality*, Lifton suggested that in China Mao was most concerned with maintaining the revolutionary fervour among those who were too young to have participated in the revolution. Ireland may be considered an example of the probability that it cannot be done. While Ireland is certainly not to be confused with China, the experiences of the post-revolutionary society indicate a movement away from revolutionary idealism to the hard facts of life: consideration of the economic situation as the primary problem seems inevitable. When such considerations clash with revolutionary goals, the revolutionary goals suffer.

But in Ireland one factor has continued to confound the political situation and makes a total break with the past very difficult. If the revolutionary goal of an 'Irish Ireland' has been displaced by more pragmatic goals, one revolutionary aim has persisted : the desire for an end of partition. Such may not have been the case had the northern situation not developed in the way that it did. But the impact of the continued disorders in the six counties since October, 1968, has dominated the political life in the Republic and brought about a severe leadership crisis in Fianna Fáil. Ministers have been forced out of the government. One has left of his own free will and left the party as well in order to form another party in the Republican tradition.

The continued problem of the North places a formidable barrier in the path that leads away from all remnants of the revolutionary period. The goal of ending partition is institutionalised in the Constitution in the beginning sections. The desire for the end of partition must still be assumed to be the credo of the contemporary Irishman.

This brings us to a rather critical point in the evolution of the Irish political elite. We have already seen that the cultural goals became secondary to those of economic growth and development. If economic well-being was dependent upon close ties with Britain then this would have to be. But the problems that continue in the North have still greater implications for the values of the Republic.

With the civil strife in the six counties, the question of partition and Protestant separation has demonstrated the need for constitutional revision, especially with regard to those aspects of Catholic social doctrine that are incorporated in the Constitution.

In Chapter 2 we suggested that a clash of values is now developing. The view that MacDonagh put forth concerning the blending of nationality and religion may have to undergo some rethinking. It has been suggested by a number of individuals that the continued incorporation of Catholic social doctrine in the Constitution stands in the way of reconciliation between the Republic and the North.

This is a most significant development. When interviews were conducted with members of the political elite soon after the outbreak of the troubles in the North, the leaders were asked specifically whether sections of the Constitution that established the special position of the Church and forbade divorce were inflammatory with regard to relations with the North. In virtually all cases the answer was that these sections were not. This series of responses was quite interesting as they were given three years after a Dáil committee on the Constitution recommended changes in the document, especially in the areas that dealt with the role of the Church.

Now that the pattern of the events in the North has become clear—that it is a community in a state of disintegration—there is a growing recognition that some accommodation with regard to the Protestants in the North needs to be made. A starting point is, very obviously, a modification of the Constitution. Religion and nationality are no longer supportive of one another; instead, one may very well be standing in the way of a realisation of the goals that the other entails.

Thus the critical problem left for the political elite is a

solution to this newest, yet paradoxically oldest, dilemma. It has taken many years to begin seeing the adherence to the Church as a barrier to a realisation of the primary institutionalised goal, the reintegration of the national territories. Yet here the transition from a revolutionary, culturally-bound elite to a post-revolutionary pragmatic group will be most telling. It is this more pragmatic group that, although less hopeful about the possibilities of ending partition, will be more realistic about those barriers which prevent unification. As was suggested earlier, the contemporary elite, regardless of party, show more features in common with one another in terms of outlook than do those revolutionary and post-revolutionary elite members of the same party. The issue of religion and nationality is just one of those areas in which that is so.

The situation in the North must continue to influence policy in the Republic. But this does not mean that because of its great concern with the problem the political elite will remain unchanged. In order to examine the Irish political elite in five years' time, the scope of this study will have to be broadened. With the passing of the revolutionary elite and with it the fairly narrow cultural nationalism of the 1920s, 30s and 40s, many of the types of constraints that hindered elite action as well as limited the types of people who would be recruited into the elite are now gone or weakened. Outside pressure groups are growing and they will have a greater impact on policy than they had in the past. Business and other economic groups will want to be heard to a much greater extent than they are now, and their influence now is not inconsiderable. Even those foreign investors who bring a large amount of capital into Ireland must be considered.

But over the past fifty years the most interesting feature of the Irish political elite has been the most inevitable, the passing of the revolutionary elite. With the emergence of the new group a new era in Irish government is apparent. It is an era punctuated by an elite that is more outward looking, more pragmatic, more sophisticated and, ironically, more 'Irish'. It is more Irish in the sense that the contemporary elite group is more representative of the population that helps to select it. What will continue to be of interest is the manner in which it meets the problem of the North, for the events there are bound to have a substantial impact on the values and policy goals of the political elite in the Republic.

NOTES

[1] Brian Farrell, 'Dáil Deputies; The 1969 Generation', *Economic and Social Review,* Vol. II, No. 3.

[2] John Whyte, *Dáil Deputies,* Dublin: Tuairim Pamphlet.

[3] J. L. McCracken, *Representative Government in Ireland: A Study of the Dáil Éireann 1919-48,* London 1958.

[4] P. Lynch, 'The Economics of Independence', *Administration,* VII (1959), 93.